THE MAN WHO FEELS
LEFT BEHIND

THE MAN WHO FEELS LEFT BEHIND

GERALD W. JOHNSON

WILLIAM MORROW AND COMPANY

NEW YORK, 1961

CONTENTS

21879

1

THE MAN WHO FEELS
LEFT BEHIND

An eminent semanticist addressing a convention of his colleagues in 1958 was quoted in the public prints to this effect:

> Man's cognizance of the immeasurable expanse of the physical universe and the infinite multiplicity of its component constituents tends to nurture a concomitant apprehension that the frontiers of verbalization are indeed coterminous with the limits of conceptual vocabulary, and that beyond these frontiers subsists a realm that defies conceptualization.

The learned doctor spoke a mouthful.

I do not refer to his sesquipedalian vocabulary. Perhaps in some Elysian mead of asphodel Quintilian stared and gasped, but if so, that is beside the point. I used "mouthful" in the vernacular sense of an utterance that is profoundly true.

For after having, in the manner of a pundit in the *Arabian Nights*, "considered for an hour," I am persuaded that what he meant is that much of great importance in the modern world is beyond words. This is profoundly true, although it is not news. In making the statement my semanticist was some nineteen centuries behind Saul of Tarsus, and several thousand years behind Prince Gautama. But while the idea is not new, the manner of approach to it is; for the semanticist attained it by aid not of intuition, but of silicon. He pursued studies based finally on microscopy and telescopy, whose instruments are glass lenses; and nobody short of a Zen Buddhist questions the tactility of a glass lens. If materiality exists, certainly glass is a material object. Yet as others through umbilical contemplation, so he through glass claims to have looked into the ineffable; and his claim is attested, in a general way, by the leaders of modern science.

They eschew the terminology of the mystics, to be sure. "Ineffable" has the status of a dirty word in the learned journals, but a man as far beyond suspicion of being a yogin as Bertrand Russell admits that certain of his mathematical statements are inexpressible in words and can be communicated exactly only by symbols. Furthermore, he approves continued research, which is to say he assumes the existence of truth not yet symbolized, much less verbalized, hence not grasped even as a concept. Lord Russell has frequently and firmly declined to set limits to the range of human intelligence, but he would hardly declare positively that no limits are conceivable, and that is not far from the position of the semanticist.

But the Deutero-Isaiah was a mystic, and to a relatively unlettered layman there seems to be a striking correspondence between what the scientists are saying and his assertion that, "since the beginning of the world men have not heard, nor perceived by the ear, neither hath the eye seen, O God, beside thee, what he hath prepared for him that waiteth for him."

So to the untutored mind it appears that physics as a part of modern science, after a march of five hundred years, taking the Revival of Learning as its point of departure, has circled around until it has arrived at the point reached by metaphysics, or superstition, twenty-five centuries ago. The vaunted progress of the intellect has achieved a retrogression of a couple of millennia.

Philosophers and scientists may brush the idea aside as a triviality, a mere verbal play unworthy of serious consideration by men who spend their lives working at the outermost verge of modern thought; which may be true. But the nation is endowed with—or afflicted by, if you see it that way—considerable numbers of men and women whose lives are not devoted to cogitation, but to the commonplace activities involved in the day-by-day operation of our political and social system, but who nevertheless aspire to formulate some kind of philosophy of life. Shallow that philosophy may be, but comprehensible it must be; and as things stand there is none available. Like an old-time cavalryman whose horse was shot under him, the intelligent but untutored man sees the battle of ideas whirling away toward the horizon, while he is left behind amid the wreckage of exploded theories and a litter of axioms dead or maimed.

It is a woeful predicament, but it is going too far to assume that it should greatly concern the heavy thinkers of science and philosophy, the Einsteins and Heisenbergs and Heideggers, or even that putative philosopher, the exotic M. Sartre. They have other fish to fry. Yet it has concerned some of them, notably Einstein, if only for statistical reasons. Those people who feel left behind may not carry very heavy intellectual armament, but they are like the grasshoppers for numbers and to a large extent they control the environment in which scientists and philosophers must exist.

This is not unimportant with respect to the advance of science and philosophy. Ultimate truth, to be sure, is not determined by popular vote, but the ultimate fate of the truth seeker may be. It is certain that no further investigations were made by Socrates after he drank the hemlock, by Archimedes after he met the legionnaire's sword, by Bruno after he went to the stake. Public opinion, although it cannot discover, can inhibit discovery, not necessarily by the stake, the thumbscrew and the rack; psychological instruments of torture will serve the purpose. McCarthyism neither burned nor beheaded a single martyr. Its sole weapon was the creation of an unfavorable climate of opinion; but it harassed and hampered the scientific community far more effectively than did those Fundamentalists who put through the Tennessee "monkey law" thirty years earlier.

It would seem, then, that it is not in the public interest for those large numbers of Americans who are intelligent without rating as intellectuals to feel left behind. But who is to convince them that the feeling is illusory? Manful efforts are being made by some of the heavy thinkers. Niebuhr and Oppenheimer come to mind at once, and of course there is the hard-fighting battalion of the popularizers, led by Eddington and Jeans and supported by such irregular auxiliaries as Joseph Wood Krutch explaining the geology of the Grand Canyon, and Edmund Wilson the exegesis of the Dead Sea scrolls. But these are not enough. They dissipate suspicion that our state is due to the Treason of the Clerks, but they do not dissipate suspicion of intellectualism. McCarthy is dead, but to assume that McCarthyism died with him is reckless optimism.

These pages, accordingly, are presented not as a contribution to the extension of knowledge, but in the hope, none too bright, that they may aid in some slight degree the control of emotion. The basic hypothesis of the work is that the man who feels left behind may attain a satisfactory *katharsis* by other and less expensive means than cracking the Egghead. The learned and the austerely rational may pass it by, for it is not addressed to them, but to the American citizen whom Fate has permitted—or sentenced— to live in the latter half of the twentieth century, but whose capacity for feeling is appreciably greater than his capacity for mastering ideas just rising above the intellectual horizon, but which nevertheless seem to have a dreadful intimacy with our everyday lives.

How may an American go about his lawful occasions unperturbed in the hour when science and philosophy seem to be dissolving the foundations of the world? The classical answer is, of course, to vegetate. That answer has sufficed in the past. The intellectual labors of Pythagoras, for example, did not perceptibly affect the existence of the contemporary turnip and the ordinary Greek. Hero of Alexandria built a steam engine in the third century, A.D., but it had no effect on the life of George Washington.

Copernicus could withhold his revelations for thirteen years, until the approach of death assured him of immunity from the chastisement of massed stupidity, and the delay made little difference. When the lag between discovery and application was measured in generations or centuries, there was no occasion for the ordinary man to become excited over the activities of advanced thinkers. But atomic fission was first accomplished in 1937 and the atomic bomb exploded in 1945; in modern times application treads upon the heels of discovery.

In the presence of the new learning, therefore, the life of the vegetable is no longer a practicable recourse for anyone. A concept that may in the course of a few generations revolutionize man's thinking about the universe and his place in it may be ignored with relative safety by the unlearned; but a concept that is liable at any moment to convert the unlearned into a wisp of radioactive vapor is a different matter. A philosophy that may in time undermine social institutions may be left to the rising generation; but one that may cast this present generation into slave-labor camps, if not into gas ovens, demands prompt attention. The thinking of a modern Pythagoras is capable of bringing swift and irretrievable ruin upon turnips and perioeci; so it cannot be ignored.

Unfortunately, it cannot be understood, either. To imagine that any considerable proportion of the American electorate will ever master even the rudiments of nuclear physics, of the algebras and geometries on which it is based, or of the philosophic concepts to which it gives rise—or, more exactly, toward which it impels—is idle dreaming. We are left behind, and the possibility that we shall catch up before

the passing of the contemporary generation is about equivalent to the theoretical possibility that two solids will pass
through each other because none of their atoms will come
into collision.

The problem of the modern American, therefore, is the
problem of dealing intelligently with what he does not
understand. At first glance this appears to be a flat impossibility, but momentary reflection is enough to dissipate that
impression. Far from being impossible, it is a commonplace
of everyday life. It is not necessary to understand thermodynamics in order to be able to drive an automobile, for
efficient controls have been devised, so simple that monkeys
can learn to operate them. The problem is thus reduced
from the impossibility of mastering all knowledge to the
practicality of devising controls that are within the comprehension of the ordinary mind.

This is not one of the labors of Hercules and it calls for
no Herculean intellect. The requisite is ingenuity rather
than profundity, which removes it from the realm of the
geniuses and brings it within the purview of ordinary people.
The exploration of outer space and the ontological aspects,
if any, of the principle of indeterminacy are matters on
which we must consent to be guided by the best scientific
and philosophical opinion available; but when it comes to
deciding what is a reasonable line of conduct for an ordinary
American under existing conditions, there is no more reason
to look to the profound thinkers for advice than there is to
call in an Einstein when your automobile engine's feed line
clogs. It would be a mistake to do so; for the chances are
that any competent garageman will know better what to do
than an Oppenheimer or a Heisenberg would. For the

learning appropriate to this case is not mastery of advanced science but knowledge of how Joe Doakes, typical citizen, is likely to act under given conditions.

But—and here is the catch in it—to choose a reasonable line of conduct one must know what existing conditions are. This is the copious fountain of the unscholarly American's woe, because much of the newly discovered truth about very great magnitudes and very small ones is in flat contradiction of common sense. A plain man deprived of his reliance on common sense is in a parlous state indeed, for he has no other guide. He is not only left behind, he is left far from home, at sea without compass or sextant or chronometer, and with clouds concealing sun and stars.

This mystification is behind the revolt against the intellectuals that has made the judicious grieve in recent years, especially when it assumes such forms as requiring college teachers and students to swear fantastic oaths, and depriving the government of the services of a great scientist because, many years ago, he kept the wrong mistress. True, bedeviling the academicians and enacting into law that gentlemen shall prefer blondes are annoyances rather than grave menaces; but the suspicion of learning that encourages the annoyances is sinister.

Thus, when the typical American feels left behind his uneasiness is more than merely his hard luck. It is a threat to science and philosophy, especially in a democracy in which political authority is exercised by the majority. It is the state of mind that in the past has produced the hemlock and the cross, the *auto-da-fé*, the pillory, and the branding iron. For newly discovered truth, by reason of the fact that it has been hitherto unknown, must at its first appearance bear the semblance of an outrageous lie. Thus at a time of intellectual ferment, when research is extremely active and prolific of results, the man of moderate intellectual attainments is subjected to a drumfire of apparent lies that will overwhelm him unless he makes a manful effort to maintain his balance and steady his judgment.

The third quarter of the twentieth century is obviously such a period. Its gross effects—military insecurity, economic uncertainty, social unrest—are staple topics of conversation everywhere. But there is a subtler, or perhaps merely a deeper, anxiety of which these are surface manifestations. It results from the discovery by millions that the larger part of what they thought they knew is simply not so. The natural response to this is not to believe anything except what is obviously, immediately, and materially profitable to believe.

This is cynicism, a tenable philosophy, but dreary, hence one that reasonable men accept only as a last resort. For one thing, it spells the death of serious effort to improve the art of government, which is to say it means abandonment of the great experiment started in 1776 and continued with remarkable success for nearly two hundred years. For this experiment, although it was initiated and has since been guided by great men, is actually the achievement of mediocre minds. Washington, Jefferson and Hamilton at the beginning, and Lincoln, Wilson, and the Roosevelts in later years, were extraordinary persons, gifted with talents rarely bestowed upon anyone, certainly not claimed by you and me. But the power actually wielded by each was derived from the support of millions of ordinary men, who participated in greatness by recognizing it. When that support is not forthcoming genius, even of the highest order, is impotent.

This is what makes it no insolence but a duty for the relatively unschooled American to do a certain amount of meddling with high matters which he can understand imperfectly at best, and which he can never hope to master. This is risky. There can be no doubt about that. Interference in important matters by people who do not understand has brought more trouble upon the world than all its studied, deliberate wickedness; for nine tenths of what we usually regard as wickedness is actually the work of some well-meaning fool who didn't know what he was doing.

But the American must assume the risk because he has assumed the right of self-government and the risk is inseparable from it. To be free has always been, is now, and ever will be dangerous; so if we insist on being free, it is puerile to blench at danger. We have contrived to face it, and face it down, for a hundred and seventy-five years, so why begin cowering now? True, the perils confronting us today are more difficult to understand, therefore more alarming than an Englishman in a red coat, or a Confederate in a gray; we are not even sure that they are summed up in a bewhiskered Communist with a bomb. Which is all the better cause for examining our predicament realistically.

It may be objected that realism implies the application of common sense and the source of our woe is the discovery that common sense is no longer to be relied on in a realm whose basic equation is $E = mc^2$ if E is energy, m is mass, and c is the speed of light—a pure negation of common sense. But there are guides and guides, and one that is utterly useless in the mazes of nuclear physics may be perfectly competent to direct us to the post office. Neutrons and electrons may elude even Heisenberg, but Republicans and Democrats are still fairly predictable, and it is with these that we are called on to deal.

This book, in fact, is written in the belief—based, perhaps, more on reasoning by analogy than on austere logic—that common sense has not been invalidated, but defeated by being misapplied. If that is the case, then the man who feels left behind is perhaps not so far behind as he is inclined to think; for the obvious perils of the republic may be susceptible of an interpretation that makes the opportunities they represent at least equal to the calamities they may portend.

A very long time ago a man who found himself in a jam somewhat resembling ours figured a way out. "Give thy servant," he prayed, "an understanding heart to judge thy people, that I may discern between good and bad." That was common sense; yet it has since been accounted wisdom of so high an order that it led not merely to national security, but to riches and honor as well.

2

THE CONQUEST OF INNER SPACE

IT is difficult to imagine the temerity that would accuse a great scientist of being a sensationalist, but it is true that in 1958 Dr. Robert Oppenheimer published in the relatively austere pages of *Harper's* an article that in effect, if not in phraseology, was as sensational as anything that it has entered into the mind of yellow journalism to conceive.

As a mere aside, in passing on to another subject, Dr. Oppenheimer remarked that the greater part of all that is now known was not in any book when he went to school; which is to say that he obtained, of necessity, the greater part of his education outside the classroom. Of course we all learn more from experience than from formal study, but Oppenheimer had in mind the intellectual, not the emotional nor the physiological content of knowledge. That is obvious because he went on to say that, beginning with Leucippus, who propounded the atomic theory twenty-five centuries ago, of all the men who have made really great contributions to physical science, ninety per cent were still living when Oppenheimer wrote. (Albert Einstein died soon after the article appeared.)

Consider if you please what these statements appear to do to the debate, as acrimonious and inconclusive as it is interminable, among the adherents of various pedagogical theories. From Pestalozzi—nay, from Montaigne, from Plato —to John Dewey, it would seem that they have been arguing over the best method of doing very little, since ninety per cent of what they are supposed to impart is not in their possession anyhow.

Consider, too, where they leave a man in middle life— Oppenheimer's age in 1958—to say nothing of one who is older. If most of what is now known was not in any book when he went to school, certainly it was not there when his seniors sat in the classroom, nor those who are slightly his juniors. Some of us who are only too well aware that our education is scanty and bad had attributed the deficiency to the fact that we didn't study hard enough in school and college. But this deliverance puts a different aspect upon the matter. No matter how hard we might have worked, we couldn't have acquired much knowledge because it wasn't available at the time. On the face of it, we never had a chance; we were left behind before the race began.

This is discouraging; but it is on the face of the facts, and one item of information that some of us did pick up from our primitive schooling is that the words "fact" and "truth" are not synonymous. Fact is the foundation of truth but the foundation only; the significance of the fact is the super-structure. A fact without significance is a part, not of truth but of pedantry, a very different thing.

Oppenheimer's statement, in short, is quantitative, not qualitative. It is probably a fact that most of what is now known was not in any book when he and I went to school;

but the significance of the fact is that most of what is now known is highly specialized knowledge of no use whatever to anyone but a specialist.

This throws a different light on the subject. A man who has acquired information sufficient to his own purposes is not left behind in any significant sense. The crucial question is not, How much do you know? It is, What do you know? The answer is reassuring or the reverse according to your own position in life. Everything depends on what you have to do. If you are required to design a chicken coop, the essential technical knowledge is not extensive; but if your task is to design a sputnik, the requisite technical knowledge is so vast that no one brain can encompass it all. Feats of that kind are successfully accomplished only by teams of highly trained technicians.

Fortunately, we can leave such operations as putting satellites into orbit around the moon to organizations of men who have devoted their lives to acquiring the necessary knowledge. But the authority to decide whether or not to perform the operation cannot be delegated. Unfortunately for him, the ordinary, multitudinous American, incapable of penetrating the mystery of a slide rule, to say nothing of the Theory of Groups, is compelled by unreasonable Destiny to make decisions for which he needs knowledge that was not in any book when he went to school, and in fact is not in any book yet.

Should we, for instance, buy manganese in Baku when we can get it in Bombay or, for that matter, in Virginia or Colorado? This is apparently a business question. It is a problem whose solution calls for no mastery of the use of tensors, nor for the ability to translate Urdu. The basic considerations are simple enough—they are the quality of the manganese and the price demanded. If both are satisfactory, we should buy from anybody who is willing and able to deliver the goods.

But just try it. Instantly you will run into a tangle of diplomatic and economic relations that might—and, in point of fact, did—bewilder Einstein. Baku is Soviet territory. Soviet Russia is the implacable foe of our whole way of life. In any fair deal both parties profit. If the Soviets profit, they will become stronger. On the other hand, if we churlishly refuse to deal when they offer a good article at a fair price, to that extent we justify their hostility at a time when it is urgently necessary to reduce tensions among the nations.

In short, an apparently simple, straightforward business transaction today involves a host of those "imponderables" that Bismarck said may affect history more than either wealth or military power. And the final decision rests, not with a Secretary of State, nor with a Doctor of Science, but with a plain businessman intent only on making a living, not on ruling the world.

Nor does American responsibility stop with industrialists and financiers on the policy-making level. Every mechanic, every white-collar worker, every housewife, and schoolteacher, and grocer, and physician, and preacher has a vote and the duty to cast it in every election for the candidate and the party that seem most likely to conduct public affairs with due regard for the imponderables. Which means that every election involves judgments in the fields of ethics and logic—fields not a whit less thorny than mathematical topology or the grammar of Hittite.

This is the consideration that appals the ordinary citizen and plunges him into a pessimism that cannot be neutralized by unexampled prosperity and military power so vast that it has only one possible rival in the world. His melancholy is all the darker not only because the information that he needs is in scanty supply in books, but also because nobody seems to be making a serious effort to supply it. He needs must proceed with what he has; and his immediate problem is to examine what he has, to evaluate it, and to stretch it as far as it will go.

It is not that he suffers from any lack of information; it is the information he needs that is missing. As for other information, it is poured upon him more lavishly than ever before in history. Not only are the book-stores loaded with innumerable tomes filled with the new learning, but the casual reader cannot pick up a newspaper or magazine without encountering a story about satellites, rockets, lunar photographs, radiation belts, or some related subject. A new demigod is in the making, outranking Achilles and rivaling Hercules. He is called the Astronaut.

But what does it mean? They say that it is the first chapter of the story of the conquest of outer space, but that is an answer satisfying to nobody but technicians. What does it mean to the ordinary man, unskilled in astronomy, mathematics, or physics, and yet responsible as a voting citizen of this republic for the activities of the scientists and engineers employed by the nation, which is to say, by the people of the United States?

To him, the only imaginable reason for the conquest of outer space is that the confines of the terrestrial globe and its surrounding atmosphere have become too restrictive for something. Obviously this is not anything to be apprehended by ordinary sensory perception. The handful of small objects that have been chemically propelled into the void are admittedly nothing more than experimental gadgets, sent out to test conditions and supply the data needed for intelligent planning of the real invasion. What is irresistibly expanding into the interplanetary abyss is obviously not to be defined in three-dimensional terms. All, said the Greek philosophers, is subsumed in number, weight and measure. But not this. Yet it cannot be ignored by any rational man because the best-informed scientists tell us that one of this expansion's incidental side effects may be the extermination of the human race, if not of all life on the planet. Above all, it cannot be ignored by any American because at least half of the work is being carried on in our name, with our money, and with our formal approval.

What has become too expansive for the whole terrene area and is now surging beyond it is not the group of small metallic containers crammed with mechanical instruments, now sent wandering between the planets, but the mind that contrived and dispatched these objects. Russell makes the questionable assertion that we are equal to all that we can understand; which implies that our reach extends far beyond the orbit even of the satellite that the Russians are presumed to have put to circling around the sun. And in the other direction it plunges below the depths penetrated by the electronic microscope.

Philosophical mathematics is now working seriously on the theory that there are entities whose dimensions are smaller than the wave length of light. They are therefore forever beyond observation and whatever properties they may have are incapable of discovery by observation. Yet they are not necessarily beyond cognition because the range of inference is as much greater than that of the electronic microscope as it is beyond that of the two-hundred-inch telescope. Toward the infinite and toward the infinitesimal, it reaches farther into outer space than any instrument that technology has created; and inference is nothing tangible, it is merely a function of the mind.

"What song the sirens sang, or what name Achilles assumed when he hid among the women, though puzzling questions, are not beyond all conjecture," thought Sir Thomas Browne, but whose bones filled the ossuary he was then contemplating he believed to be an impenetrable mystery. It was a curious blunder for so learned a man. The sirens' song is given in the *Odyssey*, and modern antiquarians are full of information about the people who practiced urn burial. The name of the disguised Achilles, it is true, has yet to show up on scroll or stele, although it may do so any day. Yet mystery has not been banished from the world.

"Why do you climb a mountain?" someone asked the conqueror of Everest, and his answer was, "Because it is there."

If Sir Thomas were writing today he might find in the interpretation of that answer a real mystery; for what made Hillary climb is the same force that impelled Russian pioneers to photograph the back of the moon. There is the invader of outer space, not the toys thrown into orbit; just as it was not the grenade that assassinated the Austrian Archduke and exploded the world in 1914, it was the man who threw it.

So much is plain even to the American who cannot manage a slide rule; from which it should be plain that the new learning that has left him behind is concerned, after all, with what the medieval philosophers termed "secondary causes." So it is possible that his bewilderment and fright are really of secondary importance compared to his knowledge, or lack of it, of primary things.

There is no real reassurance in this but it does in some degree dissipate the impression of solitude, and the thought of being left solitary appals any gregarious animal. Dr. Oppenheimer knows a vast number of things that are utterly beyond my comprehension; but he knows no better than I do why a man must climb a mountain or invade outer space simply because it is there, and it is possible that this is a kind of knowledge more to be desired than familiarity with the height of galactic space or the depth of the atom. While one is permitted to think so, the predicament of being left behind is not unbearable, for one can assuage it with the comforting irrelevance, "Aren't we all?"

On the other hand, this same argument throws upon the relatively uneducated a terrific load of responsibility. We are in no way accountable for the development of the Intercontinental Ballistic Missile, or for explaining the behavior of the electron. We lack the intellectual endowment for the exploration of outer space, infinite or infinitesimal; but as regards this inner space, the length and breadth and depth of the human personality, you and I are as well equipped to explore it as Heisenberg or Russell. We may be better equipped, for a man who has devoted a lifetime to the investigation of physics may have no energy left for dealing with metaphysics. Human resources, after all, are not without limit.

Three of the four great mysteries that puzzled Solomon have been almost completely illuminated by knowledge acquired since his day. Aerodynamics, hydrodynamics, and the coefficient of friction have revealed much about the way of an eagle in the air, the way of a ship in the sea, and the way of a serpent on a rock; but as regards the fourth and darkest mystery of them all, the way of a man with a maid, remarkably little of real significance has been learned since Adam delved and Eve span.

It is true that the scientific mode of investigation has been pursued vigorously and with considerable success. *How* a man carries on with a maid we understand now to an extent and with a precision that sometimes inhibits the operation; but *why*, psychology has not yet told us. Probably it never will, for the *why* is not embedded in the media that we call time and space, through which science operates. Sunk in an abyss it may be, but not in the abyss between the stars, nor in that between the electrons. To offer as an answer, "the perpetuation of the species," is the fallacy of *petitio principii*, "begging the question," in that it assumes that the perpetuation of the species is desirable, which is not yet proved.

Even if it were proved, the method of perpetuation is attended by circumstances of what seems to be ruthless and aimless cruelty, such as persuaded Alcidamas to put into the mouth of Homer the observation that "for men on earth 'tis best never to be born at all; or being born, to pass through the gates of Hades with all speed." Father, mother, child, all are so plainly victims that in more than two millennia logicians have never been able to refute the maxim. Yet it is out of this bitter jest that, sometimes directly, more often by a long and devious process, man has contrived to distill all of his art, most of his philosophy, and much of his religion—that is to say, all that distinguishes him from the rest of the brute creation and makes him *homo,* sometimes *sapiens,* the wise, and always *faber,* the maker.

All of which is not mere rumination, but bears directly upon the problem of whether to support X or Y in the Senatorial primary, and whether to vote Democratic or Republican in the ensuing election. For it is a kind of investigation that no self-governing people can delegate to the Chaldeans and soothsayers, whether scientific, scholastic, or theological. It must be undertaken by ordinary men and women who have learned no more than what was in books long before Oppenheimer went to school.

Failure to acknowledge this necessity and face up to it is unquestionably one of the malaises that afflict the United States in the second half of the twentieth century, and it may be plausibly argued that it is the basic ill from which all the rest derive. It is the evil popularly known as passing the buck, readily identified when it appears in the army, in politics, and in business, but not so easily spotted in philosophy because the typical American rarely thinks of himself as a philosopher, restricting that title to members of learned societies.

Passing the buck is handing on to some other authority, higher, lower, or equal, but in any case other, a decision that it is your business to make. As touching extraneous circumstances, it is only too familiar and all join in con-

THE CONQUEST OF INNER SPACE

THE CONQUEST OF INNER SPACE

demning it; but as touching thought and opinion, when it is recognized at all it is frequently defended as meritorious. Why should a man form, much less express, an opinion on a subject about which he knows nothing? The temptation is strong to answer, without qualification, he shouldn't. But there is a qualification. If the subject is one about which nobody knows much, yet on which action is inescapable, it is passing the buck not to make one's best guess and act on it. Remember the resounding words of the dissent in *Abrams v. U.S.:* "Every year if not every day we have to wager our salvation upon some prophecy based upon imperfect knowledge." Holmes is usually described as defending the right of freedom of opinion, but his words are "we have to," a locution that refers never to a right, but always to an obligation. Freedom of opinion is a duty from which the individual can be relieved only by his certain awareness that an advisor has superior information not available to him.

As regards the way of an eagle in the air, every veteran pilot, to say nothing of designers of planes, possesses knowledge that is beyond a doubt superior to that of most of us, so on that matter the opinion of the expert should control action. On the interpretation of the Dead Sea scrolls, the opinion of a skilled orientalist should be accepted by people who know nothing of Aramaic. There is no rational argument in support of our duty to form an opinion on such matters. But as regards the way of a man with a maid, the Air Force Chief of Staff and the most learned of savants are as much at sea as you or I.

Furthermore, if we really penetrated that mystery we should know a great deal more about a man's reaction to other emotional stimuli—we should have a much better idea of his way with a pimp, with a poltroon, with a hero, with a martyr. We could predict with some assurance emotional and esthetic responses and moral judgments that at present elude us. We should, in fact, be taking the first steps toward the conquest of inner space, steps comparable to producing in outer space a collision of a satellite with the moon, and the collision of a gamma-ray particle with a nucleus.

But it isn't to be done with the instruments and techniques of science. The proportion of larceny in the soul of Candidate X is not measurable with a micrometer, nor will any spectroscope disclose the yellow streak in Candidate Y. Nevertheless, such measurements control, or should control, the overt act that takes place in the voting booth; hence we are under the necessity of making them as best we can with such facilities as we are able to command. It follows that the development of our facilities is an inescapable obligation upon every citizen, and not upon scientists alone.

Yet in recent years no perceptive observer of American affairs has failed to comment on our disposition to ignore this obligation. The pious call it moral deterioration. The Freudians call it the father-image. Riesman calls it other-direction. Cynics call it the ineradicable boobishness of the boobs. But all agree that its conspicuous manifestation is a growing tendency on the part of the typical American to evade or avoid independent thought and to accept what passes for expert opinion not only in fields where it may be valid, that is, in the exploration of outer space, but also in those where *expertise* does not exist—in what for convenience may be termed the exploration of inner space.

There is, for example, continuous and clamorous debate

over whether or not the United States of America as it is presently constituted has a chance to survive. This is obviously a question on which expert opinion alone carries much weight, and the experts, differing in detail, are at one in asserting that the answer depends largely upon our success in recruiting allies. But remarkably little attention has been paid to the question of whether there is any valid reason for this country to survive. A reason, to be valid, must be one that will appeal to our potential allies, so maintenance of the American standard of living may be dismissed. An Englishman or a Frenchman, to say nothing of a Pakistani or a Burmese, cannot be expected to assume risks to maintain the American standard of living. Some other inducement must be offered.

We produced an excellent and, for the time being, an effective one in the Marshall Plan, and one rather more enduring in Truman's Point Four, the offer of technical as well as financial aid to the have-not nations. But both were temporal and spatial or, if you choose, temporary and material. Within ten years, time ran out on the Marshall Plan, leaving it no longer potent; and it will eventually run out on Point Four. But in the life of a nation, a decade is a brief interval and a century is no great matter. When these two expedients lose their value, what will be left?

Any answer that science and technology offer must be at best contingent. Circumstances may arise to make our wealth and ingenuity so valuable to the rest of the world that it will assist our defense in its own interest. But circumstances of that kind may not arise. In that event, when the time comes as we expect it to come when other nations will no longer stand in desperate need either of our money or of our skill, with what then shall we acquire allies? What national aim, what purpose, has the United States that may appeal so strongly to a foreigner as to make him deem it to his interest to accept risks in our behalf?

This question cannot be answered by the President and the Secretary of State; nor by the Joint Chiefs in the Pentagon; nor by Dr. Oppenheimer and his colleagues in the laboratories and the universities. It can be answered in part by Congress, but only as Congress is authorized and directed to answer by the American people. In the end it comes back to you and me and the man next door; for aims and purposes pertain neither to the electrons nor to the galaxies, but to the hearts and minds of men and women.

It takes an officer of great military skill to determine in advance how the power of destruction may most effectively be wielded against an armed enemy. It takes a diplomatist of equivalent skill to decide correctly what will be the effect on the international situation of our support of the claims of Nation *A* as against those of Nation *B*. But neither strategy nor diplomacy can give a conclusive answer to the first question posed by any prospective action, namely, Is it right? In an autocracy that is a question for the autocrat and for him alone. In modified autocracies—oligarchies and aristocracies—it is a question for the few in positions of authority. But in a democracy it comes straight back to the people, and if they evade or avoid it, they abdicate.

Yet the answer, by whatever authority made, is contingent. Right for what? What is right for one purpose is always calamitously wrong for another. Thus the policy, the long-range policy, of the United States will contribute to our national security in precisely the measure that the long-range purposes of that policy are approved by other nations that are in position to assist us.

Once upon a time we had such a purpose. We have never formally repudiated it, and to this day we render it lip service; but our critics aver that it is only lip service, no longer a motive controlling national action. That purpose is stated in the Declaration of Independence in the assertion that this government was established to secure to its citizens three rights, to wit, life, liberty and the pursuit of happiness. Seven years of desperate and at times seemingly hopeless fighting attested that the stated purpose was in fact our aim; and it gained the well-nigh universal approbation of mankind.

It still commands approbation. The question is not as to the purpose. Our critics do not challenge it; they merely assert that we no longer adhere to it. So if we can successfully refute that criticism there is every reason to believe that we can still rally to our side forces sufficient to neutralize any possible threat and to make our national security unquestionable.

But this we have not done in recent years. Communist charges that we are actually motivated by the smash-and-grab philosophy of the old imperial systems do not fall to the ground by reason of their palpable absurdity. On the contrary, as thoroughly American a critic as Riesman ruefully admits that appearances are against us because most Americans have submitted to other-direction and are no longer dominated by the inner drive to secure their inalienable rights.

The evidence is not to be dismissed with a shrug. It is too weighty. But granting that the condition exists, it does not follow that we are compelled to accept the explanation of the pietists, the Freudians, or the cynics. Perhaps the symptoms may be accounted for without diagnosing moral degeneracy, extreme neurosis, or irremedial stupidity in the American populace. Possibly it is mere bewilderment, attributable to that feeling of being left behind. In that case, it is in order to inquire whether we are in fact left behind or have only been confused by the whirlwind speed of travelers whom we have encountered, but who are actually going in another direction to attain a different goal.

If there is evidence to support that theory a good deal of our anxiety is baseless or misdirected; for on that theory we can leave the devotees of science to their own devices while we serenely go about ours. If they seem likely to disappear over our intellectual horizon, what of it? They are probing the outer space measured by the capacity of the mind of man. The task for which we are better fitted, the task for which we are at all fitted, is that of probing the inner mystery of his emotional nature.

For the evidence, already massive and increasing daily, is that unless the two are properly adjusted to each other they will subject the world to torsion that will twist it into monstrous shapes and probably bring it to disaster. Fifty years ago this was apparent only to exceedingly wise men, who are always few; but today it is plain to anyone capable of reading a newspaper. When the magnificent scientific culture of Germany results in producing Nazism; when the overthrow of Russian czardom eventuates in communism; and when the American experiment in self-government bears fruit in McCarthyism and thought police, Simple Simon as well as Socrates can perceive that it is a badly distorted world.

The devil, the father-image, the idiot, any or all of them may be responsible, and if so perhaps the theologians, the psychiatrists, and/or the satirists may eventually snap us out of it. But there remains the uncomfortable suspicion that none of these may be as debilitating a force as the failure of the typical American to retain the political maturity that he exhibited in the early days of the republic.

The Declaration of American Independence, written in 1776, and the Constitution of the United States, written in 1787, were productions of adult minds. But they are nearly two hundred years old, and our political philosophy should be far in advance of both by this time. In two respects it is. Chattel slavery is no longer tolerated as a legal institution, and assassination, under the euphemism of the *code duello*, is no longer admissible as a political argument. These are gains, but somewhat meager gains as the harvest of nearly two centuries.

On the other hand, as regards fealty, courage, and magnanimity, there is all too much evidence that our movement has been toward the rear; and all these are emotional, not intellectual qualities. But reliable formulae for the production of loyalty, boldness, and generosity are not in any book written before or since Oppenheimer went to school.

3

MESOPOTAMIA, SHIBBOLETH, ET CETERA

THE old lady who rose in the experience meeting to thank a gracious Providence for giving us that blessed word "Mesopotamia" was not in fact much nuttier than most of us. Her aberration showed because it was different in phrasing from yours and mine, but that it deviated any further from right reason is, to put it mildly, debatable.

For man shall not live by bread alone, but mostly by catchwords, as Robert Louis Stevenson noted. If our sustenance is not Mesopotamia, it is some shibboleth whose correct enunciation passes one without further question into the ranks of Gilead, while any undue sibilance will be taken as conclusive proof of subversive tendencies. If, for instance, you call Chinese communism a conspiracy, you are among the elect; if you call it agrarian reform, you are among the damned; and the fact that it is neither, like the flowers that bloom in the spring, tra-la, has nothing to do with the case. This passes beyond any legitimate use of words as symbols and becomes a form of incantation, a sort of verbal magic in which mere utterance becomes an effective cause.

In recent years, specifically since the Second World War, one of the most familiar of these esoterica is "leadership," most often used negatively. Pundits of every sect constantly assure us that ills of the most varied types are attributable to our lack of leadership. It is true enough, in the literal sense; but it is much like explaining that a sick man's illness is due to his lack of health. Assuredly, effective leadership has been missing in the postwar period, but it does not necessarily follow that this indicates any scarcity of leaders. Effective leadership is a compound of two elements, a leader and a following; in the absence of either, effective leadership does not exist. Where followers are not to be found, a nation may have more leaders than an alligator has teeth and yet suffer lack of leadership—as in 1840 (let's keep contemporary politics out of this) when the Whigs, with Henry Clay and Daniel Webster both available, nominated William Henry Harrison and ended with John Tyler.

That this has been our situation of late may be argued as plausibly as that the nation is denuded of leaders; and if it is true, then the emphasis that current educational policy places on training for leadership may be misplaced. It could be that training for followership is the more urgent need.

This is not altogether a play on words. True it is that a really well-equipped leader is always an admirable follower, just as, according to military theorists, the ideal second lieutenant is the best man-at-arms in his platoon; but it is easily possible for educational policy to overlook this qualification. There is persuasive evidence that we have overlooked it, particularly in that educational policy that extends far beyond the schools to include the press, the pulpit, the forum and all other factors that strongly influence public opinion.

The first mark of a good follower is, of course, that he knows his own banner. "Oh, say can you see . . . ?" the opening words of the national anthem do not constitute a rhetorical question. In the smoke and dust of controversy there are plenty who can't see the colors and follow any rag that chances to be flaunted before their eyes, which often reduces our national elections to Matthew Arnold's

> darkling plain
> Swept with confused alarms of struggle and flight,
> Where ignorant armies clash by night;

yet the educator—not the pedagogue only, but also the statesman, the cleric, and he whom Carlyle, not without irony, dubbed the Able Editor—who stresses this qualification is a rarity. We profess to be amazed by the discovery that the word "democracy" in the mouth of an American President means one thing, and in the mouth of a Russian dictator means another, almost if not quite the opposite thing. But why should we be amazed? Does the typical American know what "democrat" means? There is room for doubt.

This refers, of course, to the word as spelled with a lower-case "d." No man of ordinary prudence pretends to know what is a Democrat spelled with a capital "D" or what is a Republican with a capital "R." When Senator Byrd and Senator Humphrey are both Democrats, and Senator Goldwater and Senator Javits are both Republicans, it is evident that those terms are as indefinite as the word "primate," applicable equally to a gorilla and to the Archbishop of Canterbury.

The word "democrat" has had a long history and in the course of its transition from century to century and from place to place has acquired various meanings, each of which was legitimate relatively to time and circumstance. To attain a useful definition it is therefore essential to qualify it. Thus if we set before it the adjective "American" it becomes possible to frame a definition supported by formidable authority, because the American democrat has been examined by many sharp-eyed observers whose conclusions, differing in detail, are yet in the main alike enough to compose a recognizable picture.

This picture is the banner which we are all, in theory, pledged to follow. The question is, Has it been in the past, and is it being at present, put before our people consistently, truthfully, and clearly? Some presume to doubt it, and find in the doubt an explanation of our civic ills at once simpler and more inclusive than any of the theories that our people are possessed by the devil, obsessed by the father-image, or congenitally idiotic, the theories favored by the Puritans, the Freudians, and the Cynics respectively. A spearman uncertain which is his own oriflamme may be expected to act in such a way as to seem to be possessed, obsessed, feeble-minded, or all three. Apply, then, Occam's Razor, the principle that of two possible explanations of any phenomenon the simpler is more likely to be true, and the theory that the American people are merely confused becomes logically persuasive.

At the same time it becomes highly important. The dictum

attributed to Lincoln that you can't fool all the people all
the time does not exclude the possibility that you can fool
enough of the people enough of the time to ruin the country.
The posited basic perspicacity of the people is one of the
mudsills on which democratic government rests; but it is
possible to demolish the house without displacing the mudsills. A vice of liberalism is its tendency to forget what is
implied by "basic." Persuaded by ample historical evidence
that the collective wisdom of the people is greater than
that of any individual or oligarchy, liberals blithely assume
that because this wisdom always exists *in posse* it always
exists also *in esse*—and as a result, fall on their faces.

Potential wisdom becomes actual when it operates on
accurate and adequate information, not before. Jefferson,
high priest of American democracy, recognized this in his
observation that, "if a nation expects to be ignorant and
free, in a state of civilization, it expects what never was and
never will be." Yet it is so clear that a great many Americans
are grossly ignorant of the nature of democracy that some
of the keenest observers in the land have been reduced
to despair.

The reason for this condition is not far to seek. It has
been profitable to misinform the people—regularly profitable politically, and often profitable financially. The people
are the chosen victims of every charlatan bent upon obtain-
ing wealth and power without deserving either; and many
of these operators are extremely shrewd. The miracle of
America is, considering the energy, skill, ingenuity, and
numbers of the swindlers operating in public life, that their
success has been so relatively small. One is reminded of
the philosophical crook in *The Vicar of Wakefield* who con-

fessed to Dr. Primrose his astonishment that the honest farmer, whom the crook cheated as regularly as the annual fair came round, nevertheless showed up each year with his pockets full of money, while the crook was always broke. Boss Tweed, commonly regarded as the colossus of American thieves, may have robbed New York of 300 millions; but in 1878, when Tweed died a pauper in Ludlow Street jail, New York was still prosperous.

Nevertheless, since there is a first time for everything, it behooves the American democrat to take reasonable precautions against the possible complete success of the frauds; and certainly one reasonable precaution is to know the first principle of his political faith. Confidence men admit that it is all but impossible to swindle a man financially unless the man already has a touch of larceny in his soul. It is as difficult to impose a fraudulent doctrine upon a man unless that man already has a propensity to follow Chaldeans and soothsayers, rather than exponents of reality. Hence the main line of defense of our liberty is respect for reality, not only as against the myth of the divine right of kings, but as against all other fables, including those of recent origin.

One of these is the theory of equality of opportunity as characteristic of the American system. Any boy born within its limits, we say, may become President of the United States. It is not true. A boy born without enough brains to become an efficient hod carrier cannot become President. As of today, a boy born of Negro parents cannot become President. Against a boy born of Jewish parents the odds are very great, and until recently they were almost as great

against one born of white and Christian, but Roman Catho-
lic parents. There are more than five hundred boys born
every day in the United States, of whom only one can be
President at any given time. As the one elected will hold
the office a minimum of four and a maximum of ten years,
and accepting the Psalmist's life span of seventy, the choice
theoretically might fall upon seven to eighteen of those
born on a given day; but it is mathematically certain that
482 to 493 out of 500 would not have a chance even if
every one of them survived for seventy years.

The great majority, however, will survive for twenty-one
years, and of those who do, disregarding the fraction that
will lose their faculties by calamity or their civil rights by
committing felonies, all will incur the obligation of voting
for the man of their choice for President. We habitually say
"will acquire the right" to vote, but it is a bad habit; the
fact that there is no legal penalty for evading it does not
convert a duty into a right. Of a citizen of a democracy,
therefore, it may be said that while he probably will never
need to know how to lead the nation, he will certainly need
to know how to follow honest and intelligent leadership.

Where, then, shall he look for that instruction? Not to the
schools, for they are frankly—and loudly—"dedicated to
training for leadership." So are the Boy Scouts, the
Y.M.C.A., and the Junior Chamber of Commerce. So, in
fact, is everything in the nature of an agency of uplift with
the possible exception of the League of Women Voters and
an occasional neighborhood discussion group. Formal education for followership is conspicuous for its absence from
the American scheme of things, and the conscientious citi-

zen is thrown upon his own resources; which is, perhaps, not altogether to be deplored, since what a man teaches himself he does not forget.

Self-education, however, is notoriously inexact, which is no wonder, since it is a form of self-discipline, and discipline is by nature disagreeable. Lawyers exist largely because so many of us find it flatly impossible to force ourselves to read the fine print attentively, although we know that the fine print is the grass in which the snakes lurk. We read the Declaration of Independence and note its proclamation as a self-evident truth that the pursuit of happiness is an inalienable right. Physically, the words may be all the same, but psychologically "happiness" appears to us in great primer type and "pursuit" in nonpareil, or as modern printers say, in eighteen-point and six-point respectively. It should be the other way about, but only by bitter experience do we learn that truth.

Unfortunately, that is not all we learn, or think we learn. The same document informs us that all men are created equal, but the first glance around us affords ocular demonstration that all men are not equal; which teaches us what is not so, namely, that the Declaration lies and therefore is a most questionable guide in the conduct of life. But the lie is not in the Declaration; it enters when we read "created" in print so fine that it might as well not be there at all; so reading, assume that Mr. Jefferson and his colleagues guaranteed us happiness and equality.

The assumption that all men are created equal cannot be disproved, so it cannot be denounced as a lie; and it is a necessary basis of the democratic theory, so there is a legitimate reason for its presence in the Declaration. This clears it of the charge of fraud as well as that of mendacity. The equality of men as men is one of the unproved but essential suppositions on which our system of government rests. In 1776 we agreed to proceed *as if* it were certain that all men are created equal, and *as if* it were certain that they are endowed by their Creator with inalienable rights. In the absence of such an agreement democracy would not make sense.

But no supposition can stand unless it can be adjusted to conform to demonstrated truth. The demonstrated truth is that no matter how exact men's equality may be at the indeterminate moment of their creation, it does not survive beyond the moment of birth. A deformed baby is obviously not the equal of a normal one.

The practical significance of this derives from the logical necessity that when men are unequal some must be superior. But the most unpopular doctrine, the arch heresy in American political thought, is precisely the doctrine of the superior man. It is supposed to contravene our every political principle, to repudiate the intellectual heritage we have received from the Founding Fathers. So we believe, ignoring when we are not ignorant of it the agreement of Federalist John Adams and Republican Thomas Jefferson, both on the existence of the natural aristocracy, and on the desirability of submission to its rule.

Here is the baldest proof of the failure of our educational system—once more including in that term not only what Teacher writes upon the blackboard, but also what is proclaimed by pulpit, press, and forum. Of course, the failure is not complete. Our educators are but human, so they cannot always be wrong. Certain superiorities—as that of

the Rev. Billy Graham over most evangelists, that of the
eminent Floyd Patterson over most prize fighters, and that
of the beauteous Princess of Monaco over most Cinderellas
—are manifest, so much so that to deny them would be a
fatuity beyond even American education. The point too
often ignored is that the superiority in each case is selective.
Mr. Graham is not a champion heavyweight, Mr. Patterson
is not an eloquent preacher, and the Princess could not star
as either. Hence to yield precedence to a man's unquestionable superiority in one line is as sensible as it is foolish
to yield him precedence, period.

Yet this folly American education has fostered so consistently and so sedulously that today if a man demonstrates
superlative, let us say transcendent, ability in painting
barber poles, he is almost sure to be elected Mayor, and
some will propose him seriously for President. Remember—
to choose examples avoiding invidious comment upon the
living—the presidential booms of William T. Sherman and
Henry Ford. The late General Sherman acquired a reputation for eccentricity almost eclipsing his military fame, by
blasting such nonsense.

All this is so obvious that it will hardly be challenged by
any thoughtful reader of the newspapers; but its mere
statement is of small practical assistance to the man who
feels left behind and who must rely on his own efforts if
he is ever to catch up. His need is for some touchstone that
will assist him in choosing among superiorities the one most
appropriate to the immediate purpose. He yearns for some
shibboleth that will instantly and automatically mark off

the man of Gilead from the Ephraimite; and unfortunately none exists.

Yet it does not follow that his case is therefore hopeless. He has, in fact, one resource, nothing magical, and not always reliable, but one that has served well enough thus far to keep the republic from crashing into ruin. This is the quality that for lack of a really good definition we term common sense.

Its reputation at the moment is somewhat deflated. The savants who explore the outermost ranges of thought are forever coming up with some new discovery that apparently makes a shambles of common sense. The mathematicians' revelation that pq minus qp is not necessarily zero; Heisenberg's principle that a particle within the atom may be now here, and now there, without ever going from here to there; the current investigations of the hydrogen line hinting that beyond the limits of our own galaxy the concept of distance may have no comprehensible meaning; Goedel's Proof that mathematical proof does not and cannot prove—in the presence of these ideas, all at least tentatively accepted by science, to invite a man to place any reliance whatever in his common sense bears some resemblance to a bad joke.

Nevertheless, all the discoveries and inventions of modern science have not shaken one monument of common sense, namely, the determination never to cross a bridge until you come to it. In the brief span of life allotted to man most of us will never proceed so far toward the outermost boundaries of thought as to make quanta or the red shift in galactic light urgently important to us; and in the relatively tiny area of human experience nothing has materially re-

duced the value of the quality that pagan philosophers and
Church Fathers alike rated as the highest mundane virtue,
that *prudentia* which is inadequately translated by "prudence," because it includes most of what we mean by intelligence, foresight, and discretion, as well. All these are implied in the term "common sense" but *prudentia* as the first
of worldly virtues implies in addition the will to apply intelligence, foresight, and discretion.

To assert that it has not been reduced in value is to run
counter to the opinion of many worthy persons who point
out (a) that we stand in imminent danger of being
vaporized by a hydrogen bomb at any moment; and (b)
that the hydrogen bomb is the product of exceedingly ab-
struse calculations involving many of the new ideas that
apparently contradict common sense; therefore, (c) it is
nonsense to assert that the contradiction has not lessened
the value of the quality.

The flaw in this reasoning is that it disregards one of the
chief postulates, to wit, that the hydrogen bomb does not
exert enough force to break an egg as long as it remains
unexploded. The catastrophe is the explosion, and the menace is not the bomb, but that which causes it to explode;
and this cause is not the smaller atomic bomb that triggers
the hydrogen, not the sudden contact that sets off the
atomic bomb, and not the electrical impulse that brings
about the contact, but the act of will that releases the electrical impulse. This, finally, is not the will of the soldier
who, obeying orders, throws the switch. It is the will that
issues the order.

The cause of the explosion therefore is the will of the
highest authority in the chain of command. In a totalitarian

government this may be the head of the state, but in a democracy the head of the state is himself subject to the authority of the people. President Truman kept on his desk a sign reading, "The buck stops here," but the statement was only approximately correct. It may be true in all cases save those of great decisions; but in the greatest the buck is passed from the President right back to you and me.

The hydrogen bomb is therefore a menace precisely to the extent that the will to explode it is, or presently will become, irresistible in the highest authority. In the case of the American-made bomb that authority is the American people. To assume, then, that the bomb is the certain doom of mankind is to assume that the American is a reincarnation of Cain, in whom the impulse to murder could not be restrained.

This is a truth not pleasant to contemplate, so perhaps it is idle to expect orators and Able Editors to contemplate it earnestly and long. Nevertheless, it is just as the common man understands exactly where the danger lies that he will take reasonable precautions against it. A good many of the precautions suggested are anything but reasonable. For instance, Russian insistence on the immediate destruction of existing stock piles of nuclear weapons is based on the assumption that the threat is a material object. It isn't. The threat is the knowledge of how to construct the object, and knowledge can be destroyed only by destroying every brain that has mastered it. Abolishing the stock piles would accomplish nothing unless it were accompanied by the extermination of all physicists, which not even Khrushchev has proposed.

The effective will to explode a hydrogen bomb is not a

biological urge comparable to hunger and thirst. It is directed by identifiable psychic motives, the most common and most powerful of which are hatred, fear, and greed. Of these, greed is the one that is fundamental and ineradicable; hatred and fear are occasionally, although rarely, based on reasonable grounds and can be eliminated only by removing the grounds; but far more often they arise from prejudice which, in turn, is created by misinformation.

So it comes down to this: our hatred, fear, and greed, fomented and often created by our ignorance and stupidity, comprise half of the menace that hangs over the world today. The other half is comprised in the same unlovely traits in our adversaries, chiefly the Communist powers.

But is this good campaign thunder? Can any rational mind imagine a political orator, touting for votes, telling the voters that half of the terrors that fret and fever them are creations of their own stupidity and villainy? It is unimaginable and, in fact, it is undesirable. Candidates for office aspire to be agents of the people, and it is not fitting for an agent to undertake to correct the moral delinquencies of his principal. The agent should be content to devise ways and means of effecting the purpose that the principal has in mind. So much the voter is entitled to expect; but he usually gets it in scant measure, when he gets it at all.

What he is commonly given is a mixture of flattery and appeals to his pride, his prejudice, and his avarice. If the campaign orator is a competent politician, the mixture will be very skillfully blended, often so skillfully that it takes a shrewd mind to detect what is really in it. But the requisite quality is shrewdness, not prodigious learning, and a man of very ordinary intellectual capacity, by taking thought as he acquires experience, may develop a considerable, sometimes an impressive shrewdness. It is nothing unheard-of for an illiterate to hoodwink a Doctor of Philosophy; and a man of relatively little schooling may develop a political maturity proof against the wiles of Alcibiades himself. That is old stuff, common knowledge for generations, and in its age is part of its value.

For if and when the ordinary American realizes that the perils he faces in this turbulent century are perils with which he has been familiar since childhood, he may still be in dire distress, but he will not be in a dither. The horror of the times is the impression that we are in the grip of forces of incalculable magnitude whose behavior is largely unpredictable, and whose properties for the most part are not as yet ascertained. Atomic fission and fusion, radio-activity, magnetic and gravitational fields, we are told, are potencies so intimately affecting our existence in this world that they may terminate it at any time. But to most of us they are dark mysteries; for the slightest acquaintance with them we must depend upon the reports of highly trained investigators, pretty much as our ancestors a few centuries ago felt that they were dependent for their knowledge of the unseen world upon a handful of men and women who were skilled in sorcery.

If it were true that our danger arises from these mysterious sources, we should indeed be in little better case than were the jungle and desert primitives who felt that their hope of survival rested in propitiation of warlocks and witches who

knew the secret of exorcising demons. But we have co-existed
with these powers since time began, and they are not a
whit more dangerous today than they were when genus
homo first appeared upon the earth. We stand today in
precisely the danger in which Neanderthal man stood when
he faced a large enemy with a club. The club was not the
danger then, nor is the Intercontinental Ballistic Missile the
danger now; then the danger was, and now it is, murder in
the heart of the enemy.

To detect it, to neutralize it, if possible to eliminate it,
is the road to safety, and the only road. But the knowledge
required to follow that road is no discovery of yesterday.
Mastery of nonlinear equations is of no help at all in dis-
tinguishing between a scoundrel and an honest man, or
between a wise man and a jackass. Profound learning in a
narrow field may in fact be a hindrance to accurate judgment
in such matters. But in sober truth, this is no great comfort.
Few of us come to voting age without having gained some
inkling of how difficult such judgments are, and men past
ninety have confessed that they find them as difficult in old
age as they were in youth.

But they are merely difficult, not impossible. Civilization
would never have emerged had not the majority of men
been capable of making roughly accurate estimates of the
moral quality of their fellows. We are accustomed to that
sort of thing, and nobody shakes in his shoes at the thought
of trying it. We are, in fact, too confident. To calculate
the power, in megatons of TNT, of a hydrogen bomb is a
task that no rational mind would essay without long training in higher mathematics and nuclear physics. Yet it is a

relatively simple operation by comparison with the task of determining exactly how much of a blithering idiot your present member of Congress is; nevertheless, on each election day we blithely render a decision on that point. Woeful experience has taught us that we can be wrong; but to date we have been right often enough to save the country from complete disaster.

The discoveries of modern science have not created any new perils. They have merely increased somewhat the penalties that have always attached to old mistakes. No duties have been imposed upon the citizen of the United States in the twentieth century that he did not assume when he asserted his independence in 1776. The difference is that the advance of science and technology has made imperative somewhat more precision and decidedly more speed in rendering judgment.

Without doubt this is a rigorous requirement, but it is compensated in some measure by two factors—a very large increase in both the amount and the accuracy of the information available to all classes, including the lowest on the economic scale; and the spread to all classes of education sufficient, in theory at least, to render them capable of making rational use of information.

The catch in it, of course, is the catch that existed in 1776 and that will continue to exist through the predictable future. It is the incorrigible human tendency to rely, in dealing with the imponderables, more upon emotional than upon rational processes. It is a weakness that hampered grandfather and sent him to his grave owing money. It is one that probably will continue to hamper grandson even

in that millennial dawn when racial segregation shall have
been disestablished and the housing problem solved. But it
is not new. It is not mysterious. It is not beyond the comprehension and the partial control of men who went to
school as early as Oppenheimer and who learned there
even less.

It follows that the man who feels left behind flatters
himself if he assumes that he is of all men the most forlorn.
His woe arises not because the battle has swept beyond his
ken, but because of his inability to choose from a multi-
plicity of standards the one that is rightfully his. Inadequately trained in followership, he is no better prepared
than Justice Shallow for the stern demand, "Under which
king, bezonian? Speak, or die!"

In the circumstances the blessed word Mesopotamia
availeth naught, nor the pronunciation of shibboleth. But
it does not follow that the case is hopeless. The insignia and
the significance of the colors can be learned well enough for
a man to identify his own flag, if he sets to work to learn
them. But it does require work. Not by sloth, nor by effort-
less intuition, but by brisk thinking does an American voter
learn just how and when a man may smile, and smile, and
be a villain, and not in Denmark only; and it is by taking
thought that he learns how an orator may speak with the
tongues of men and of angels yet be but sounding brass or
a tinkling cymbal.

If it takes an Einstein to understand that, then most of
us are mental giants; yet its understanding is enough for
the purpose of making a good citizen in a democracy. What
remains is no more than an effort of will—that the man shall

apply his understanding to the selection of good men to conduct public affairs. Yet it must be admitted that this calls for an energy and persistence not always present in the best of men, and almost always lacking in the worthless. The possibility that it may be lacking in a majority at a critical moment is the potential cause of the explosion of the hydrogen bomb.

4

TO LIVE AND DIE
IN DIXIE

As the twentieth century swung toward its three-quarter post, the American who felt furthest behind was probably the citizen of the late Confederacy who was unfortunate enough to be able not only to read the newspapers but to understand something of what was in them.

The ability is not universal, not even, as our semanticist would say, "coterminous" with literacy. All America, but the South especially, seems to be afflicted with great numbers of citizens who apparently do their reading through spectacles equipped with lenses having a special property of fluorescence that enables the reader to detect infrared and ultraviolet where nothing appears to the naked eye except prosaic black and white.

These persons are happily free of any feeling of retardation. On the contrary, they are convinced that they move in the van of civilization and are irate when their certainty is questioned. To me they appear to be insane, but they are not unhappy, and who knows?—they may be the only sane people in a mad world. There is profound philosophical penetration in the sweet singer's immortal lines:

Observe the happy moron;
He doesn't give a damn.
I would I were a moron—
My God! Perhaps I am.

Nevertheless, irrevocably committed to the illusion that I am sane, I see in the antics of the land of my birth in recent years evidence of a cultural lag appreciably greater than that of the rest of the nation; and to say so is to accuse the South of being far behind indeed. When Eisenhower dispatched Federal troops to occupy the city of Little Rock, Arkansas, he retreated behind the year 1877, when President Hayes withdrew the last of the Army of Occupation; but Eisenhower did so because the State of Arkansas had retreated behind the year 1833, when President Jackson embalmed, cremated, and buried the doctrine of Nullification.

The genesis of this lag is easily detected. In 1868, the year of its ratification, the Fourteenth Amendment bore no more relation to the facts of human experience than the axioms of non-Euclidean geometries bear to them. The South, living of necessity in a factual world and under compulsion to adjust to nonfactual law, resorted to subterfuge as the only way out of the *impasse;* and the rest of the country, unable to devise any workable alternative, tolerated the subterfuge for many years.

But the departure from candor bore the fruit that it always bears. In the course of time the South came to believe its own bunk. The "grandfather clause" was written into the constitutions of various Southern states by men who were perfectly aware of its disingenuousness. It provided that the literacy test might be ignored if the applicant for registration as a voter was a descendant of a citizen qualified to vote before 1867, and its purpose was to disqualify illiterate Negroes—at that time, the great bulk of the Negro population—while admitting illiterate whites to the suffrage.

It was frankly a device for defeating the purpose of the Fourteenth Amendment while apparently complying with the letter of the law. In some cases the quality of this device was kept in mind, and when white illiteracy had been sharply reduced, as in North Carolina in 1908, the grandfather clause, having served its purpose, was abrogated. But in other states it remained until it was struck down by the Supreme Court of the United States. By that time, its essential fraudulence had been forgotten and it was regarded by many not as a doubtful expedient to gain time until the Negro could be prepared for full citizenship but as the embodiment of a sacred principle; to wit, the principle that the Negro should not ever be admitted to full citizenship.

Acceptance of a fraud inevitably involves some deterioration of character. In that sentence is compressed the political history of the South since Reconstruction. Its exegesis is the whole corpus of William Faulkner's work, admittedly the greatest artistic achievement of the South in this century. The tale that Faulkner tells in many volumes is that the very section in which once the concept of honor was so highly esteemed that for even a fantastic idea of honor men did not hesitate to sacrifice life itself has now accepted fraud for three generations and has become, as one critic put it, "tricky and mean." It is a tragedy worthy of the novelist's genius, tragedy on a more than epic scale.

Yet I have never encountered a white Southerner without pride in his heritage. Some no doubt exist, but they are invisible, presumably because they conceal their Southern nativity. For the rest, the danger in which they stand is not that of losing their pride of birth but that of permitting it to swell into a foolish and offensive arrogance. Men whom ambition, or economic or professional necessity, drove out of the South decades ago still tend to proclaim, rather than to conceal, their origin. Even those who fled from the intellectual sterility of their early environment realize that its emotional wealth is prodigious; they may be able to think better almost anywhere else, but nowhere else can they feel as intensely, so they are aware that their voluntary exile is far from being one hundred per cent gain.

On the face of it this is a paradox, and to resolve it should be interesting and possibly instructive. That it can be done completely is incredible, but even a partial resolution may contribute somewhat to a clearer understanding of the continental confusion that is the United States of America today.

The greatest enemy of the late Confederacy was certainly not Ulysses S. Grant, or even William T. Sherman. They were, in fact, its political and economic liberators—a trifle rough in their methods, careless of life in Grant's case, and of fire in Sherman's, but in the end highly effective. They had a job to do and they did it; the modern South has no just cause to regard either with anything but a somewhat grim yet very real respect.

Far more lasting damage was done it by men whom the South adores: at the head of the list Stephen Collins Foster, the Pennsylvania magician who betrayed the South into hugging the delusion that melody is all in all, in complete disregard of the tonic value—nay, the harsh necessity—of counterpoint. Deceivers of the same kind were orators of Henry Grady's school and a long procession of literary gents, beginning with John Pendleton Kennedy and culminating in Thomas Nelson Page.

They meant no harm and, to do them justice, they told no lies. But a lie does not have to be told; by what they did not tell these fictioneers propagated the titanic lie that Keats has preserved in the amber of great poetry:

> "Beauty is truth, truth beauty,"—that is all
> Ye know on earth, and all ye need to know.

The South believed it and, since the South is beautiful, it developed a complacency that has wreaked more permanent devastation upon it than Sherman perpetrated all the way from Atlanta to Savannah and thence up to Durham Station, where Johnston surrendered. Atlanta was soon rebuilt on a greater and finer scale; and before they died such great ladies as my old friend Mrs. MacMaster, of Columbia, had acquired other spoons. That damage was temporary. But to this day there remain far too many otherwise intelligent Southerners with an implicit faith that the beauty of the South compensates for all else that it lacks.

Precisionists will promptly argue that when these Southerners say "beautiful," what they mean is "pretty." There is some force in the objection, but not much. Even the geographical South defeats it; to call "pretty" the Valley of Virginia, or the view from Mitchell, highest peak east of the Mississippi, or old Charleston, or the enclosed gardens of New Orleans would be to perpetrate a semantic crime. The magnificence of Daytona Beach, the sullen menace of

Hatteras, the Potomac before Mount Vernon, and Old Man River himself, command reverence, not delight. Even the magnolia, which cynics have made almost a term of disdain, is superb—somewhat spectral, perhaps, but far beyond mere prettiness.

It is beauty of a different type, however, that worked the ensorcelling of the modern South and, like Vivien's spell upon Merlin, put its strong magic to sleep. It is the beauty of the legend, informing and irradiating the landscape but distorting the vision and paralyzing the will. It is the fashion of the moment to denigrate that beauty, calling it sickly sentimentalism; but beauty it was, and is, and ever will be—Circean, indeed, but real.

From Kennedy's *Swallow Barn*, to Mitchell's *Gone With the Wind*—just a hundred years apart—it has enchanted men of every section and undoubtedly will continue to enchant them as long as the telling of tales delights the human heart. It is, in fact, a recrudescence of the Arthurian legend, of loyalty, love and derring-do all compact—in short, romance. Tara and Red Rock were never built of brick and stone but of the same dream stuff that composed the walls and towers of Camelot; yet when all is said and done, it is the only building material that is utterly indestructible.

A man from Iowa or Maine can read this legendry with no sense of personal involvement, therefore with no more damage than he sustains from reading the exploits of the Round Table. Who in his right mind would seriously claim blood kinship with Gareth or Pelleas? But in the South, all this is told as of grandfather's day; it is close, it is intimate, hence the Southerner is moved by a dangerously strong impulse to maintain the legend, and "that way madness lies."

Nevertheless, the beauty is there, it is real, and it is imbued with potent sorcery. It involves the three great verities, poverty and love and war, whose acquaintance every man must make if he is to be completely educated; and no amount of abuse by the mawkish and the maudlin can destroy it. The calamity of the modern Southerner is that of Don Quixote—his wits were already lost before the curate arrived to sort out the meretricious from the sound.

But the South is in fact beautiful, whether you construe "the South" as meaning the land or the legend, and the memory of its beauty grips the emotions of its sons, no matter how long they may have been away. The misfortune is that all too many Southerners believe Keats not only when he says truthfully "that is all ye know," but also when he lies by adding, "and all ye need to know."

However, nothing absolute can be said of forty million people, not even that they all exist; for within the time that it takes to make the statement some will die and others will be born. Not all Southerners have succumbed to Vivien's spell and relatively few have succumbed entirely. O. Henry's former Confederate colonel turned editor of *The Rose of Dixie* is a recognizable type that survives to this day, but even fifty years ago his obsession with the legendary South was recognized as an oddity not to be taken seriously.

As recently as the spring of 1960, the British critic D. W. Brogan considered it worthy of note that, although when he began reading American history as a boy in Scotland he sided with the South, after he became a mature man he realized that "the right side won" the Civil War. As I am some years older than Mr. Brogan, it may interest him to learn that, as a boy in North Carolina, I heard and heeded an uncle who had served the Confederacy faithfully and well but who told me, "Yes, they had more men, and more artillery, and more rations, and more everything else, but, boy, don't you ever believe that that was what whipped us. We lost that war because God Almighty had decreed that slavery had to go."

Mr. Brogan is quite right in noting that although the legalists, citing Abraham Lincoln as their chief witness, have proved conclusively that slavery was not the issue, yet the fact remains that the war was *about* slavery because the legal issue, secession, arose out of slavery. But Mr. Brogan is quite wrong in assuming that the South had not realized that as early as fifty years ago. It was known in North Carolina that the right side won, even when boys in Scotland were still siding with the South.

The argument against the South that would be conclusive, if it were sustained by fact, is that, having appealed to the arbitrament of the sword, it refused to abide by the judgment it had invoked, and so was forsworn. But the argument is only doubtfully sustained by the fact. The undisputed fact is that the judgment was that slavery had to go, and it went. Even the furiously reviled "black codes" of Mississippi and Louisiana did not attempt to re-establish legal slavery, and were less rigorous than the *apartheid* legislation of South Africa ninety years later. If the North, victorious but stung by grievous wounds, imposed, after hostilities had ceased, new conditions not nominated in the bond, who was then forsworn? It is a pretty question, one that has given Southern casuists their opportunity.

After so many years, however, even to admit the argument to debate is casuistry in the pejorative sense. Attempts at the attribution of blame hinder, not help, the search for a solution of current problems, most of them arising from the refusal of the South to grant the Negro all the rights and privileges appertaining to the status of first-class citizenship.

Note well the phraseology. It runs "to grant him the rights," not "to recognize his status"; for the latter is a refusal based on the simple and solid fact that, taken in the mass, the Negro is not a first-class citizen. There is no convincing evidence that he is biologically inferior, but even Gunnar Myrdal admits that there is every evidence that he is culturally inferior. Two hundred and fifty years of bondage have left their mark, which ninety-five years of freedom have not erased.

The casuists of the South contend that this is in itself evidence of the Negro's irremovable inferiority. Those of the North contend as fiercely that it is evidence only of the irremediable wickedness of the white South. Both contentions are empty gabble, innocent of logical consistency or historical perspective. Logically, the existence of this republic can be justified only on the assumption that the status of a freeman is favorable to the development of political competence; were it not so, we should have done better to adhere to some other system. Historically, Runnymede, starting point of the English-speaking peoples' struggle for political liberty, is nearly seven hundred and fifty years in the past; yet he who thinks that we have perfected our competence is an optimist indeed. Shall we then brand the Negro as inferior because he has not accomplished in ninety-five years what the white man has not completed in more than seven centuries? Or shall we brand the white South as wicked because it has not performed the miracle of endowing another race with qualities it is still struggling to develop in its own character?

Citing individual exceptions is no rebuttal. Certainly to call Ralph Bunche a second-class citizen would be as preposterous as to call King Arthur a second-class Briton. Thurgood Marshall is a first-rate lawyer, Marian Anderson a first-rate artist, and so it goes down a long and scintillant roster. But these are examples of what the Negro is capable of becoming, not of what he presently is; and what he presently is determines his influence upon the situation existing here and now.

The difficulty of the South is not that it is astigmatic, but that it is not hypermetropic. It sees clearly enough what is directly before it, but its distant vision is blurred. Or let us say, abandoning the optical metaphor, that it is weak in applying the logic of its own experience to test the hypothesis now presented.

It is beyond belief that many Southerners will concede that their political history since 1776 has been so complete a failure that they have made no advance in the art of self-government. It may be admitted that they have produced no masters of the theory of government superior to Jefferson, Madison, Marshall, Clay, and Calhoun; but the masses certainly know more about the management of public affairs than their great-great-grandfathers knew, and the development of their skill they owe to long practice under political freedom.

The hypothesis now presented is that the same conditions will produce in Negroes the same effect. The method of

testing it is, of course, to proceed *as if* it were true. The
objection to applying that method is the necessity of risking
the whole social structure upon the outcome. For this a
courage is requisite that to many Southerners seems temerity
not to say foolhardiness. Their opinion is perfectly honest,
and could be correct. The sole answer to their objection
is Danton's advice to the Convention—that audacity is the
only way out.

Above and beyond all this there is a psychological, or
perhaps a biological, block ignored by the thoughtless, but
formidable nevertheless. It is the primeval impulse, not
monopolized by man but shared by bird and beast and
creeping thing, to equate "alien" and "enemy." Jeremiah,
who antedates the Confederacy by a very considerable time,
took note of the speckled bird that "the birds round about
are against her." Whatever is not of our kind is *ipso facto*
objectionable, and a definite exercise of the intelligence is
required to neutralize the repugnance. The Negro merely
by his coloration is, of all other races, the one most completely alien to the white man, hence the one surest to
arouse—and to reciprocate—this ancient hostility. The primitive or, in ordinary parlance, the "natural" relation of black
and white is one of dislike.

This is no defense but it is a partial explanation of such
policies as segregation. Morality may be defined as the
conscious suppression of destructive biological urges, and
the advance of civilization is measured by the success of
that suppression, so the appearance of any "instinctive"
reaction is a slip backward toward Neanderthal man. But
that they do appear constantly is attested by trials everywhere and every day for homicide, theft, rape, and abduc-

tion. It will be a very long time before they are eliminated. Race prejudice will not be eliminated soon; the hope is not to eliminate it but to prevent its expression in race injustice, certainly as far as the forms of law are concerned.

The theory cherished by idealists that race prejudice is exclusively the product of miseducation and bad environment is only about ninety per cent true. There is a residue that can be traced back certainly into prehistory, and the attitude of the animals toward a variant strongly suggests that it can be traced back into prehumanity. However well suppressed, the thing exists, in Detroit as certainly as in New Orleans, in Massachusetts as in South Carolina. Latent everywhere, it needs only a certain combination of evil chances to become manifest. And its existence is one more complication added to the other troubles of the South.

This adds up to a dismal sum. The odds are plainly against the South, and if the region survives as more than a mere Boeotia, as an effective participant in American civilization, it will be only by dint of bitter travail; for it contends against itself as well as against adverse outward circumstance. The passions and frailties common to all humanity are doubly dangerous to the South, made so by the peculiar course of its history; while at the same time it must contend with all the dangers and difficulties that bring woe to other regions, because they are inherent in the democratic process.

What then is the reason, if there is a rational reason, for a Southerner's pride in his birthplace? Why, its difficulties, of course.

"I," said Saint Paul when they taunted him with being a nobody from nowhere, "am a citizen of no mean city." Every

Southerner knows how he felt. We are sons of a land that has paid its way. For a century, in fact, it has been paying not only its own debt but that of the whole nation, first incurred in 1619 when that Dutch ship of evil omen cast anchor off Jamestown and, among other items, sold the Virginia colonists "twenty negurs"; and that was augmented for the next hundred years by the Middle Passage of New England shipmasters, running rum to Africa, bringing slaves to Southern ports, and thence carrying molasses to Medford to make more rum.

For their part in that crime the North and the West were let off at the price of four years of blood and agony a century ago. But the South paid that price and in addition to it ten years of military occupation, thirty years of poverty and grinding toil, ninety years of harassment, anxiety, frustration, and moral deterioration. The South has been granted no favors. The South has paid in full.

Every historian is aware that up to about the year 1900 it labored in economic thralldom under a fiscal system that exploited it ruthlessly for the profit of the industrialized sections, but that loss was merely monetary. Far more galling to intelligent Southerners has been the inevitable result of the acceptance of fraud as a legitimate device in politics. Heaven knows, fraud is no stranger to the politics of any part of the country, but elsewhere it enters furtively and is killed by exposure. It is a vice that pays to virtue the tribute of hypocrisy. But in the South the grandfather clause and, later, innumerable tricky registration laws were adopted for the open and avowed purpose of doing indirectly what the Constitution forbade being done directly. Political leaders otherwise of good repute publicly justified this

course, and in order to sustain it did not hesitate to appeal
to every villainous prejudice and passion in the lowest
elements of society.

The inevitable result was the reduction of the political
process to a level so ruffianly that it became a national
scandal—and this in the very region that in the early days
had produced more brilliant thinkers on the art of government than came from any other part of the country. The
South that had once graced the halls of Congress with
Pinckneys, Randolphs, Clays, and Calhouns now sent Heflins,
Bleases, Bilbos, and Eastlands. The South that had given
to the Presidency the Virginia Dynasty—Washington, Jefferson, Madison, and Monroe—could furnish only one
President in ninety-five years, and that one by first having
him processed by twenty years' residence in New Jersey.

The South has paid in money. It has paid in toil and
trouble and anxiety and humiliation. But it has paid in full,
and it still survives. More than that, even as it staggered
under its backbreaking load, it has accomplished a feat
unparalleled in the history of the white race. In less than a
century, it has brought a formerly illiterate and servile population numbering many millions from tutelage to a point so
close to the van of civilization that they are now ready to
assume the most difficult citizenship in the world, that of
responsible members of a self-governing nation that is also
a great power.

In this the white South did indeed have assistance, but
not from the victors of the Civil War. It was the assistance
of the Southern Negro himself, who wrought the major part
of his own transformation and therefore is entitled to the
major part of the credit. But not to all. The ignorance,

prejudice, and stupidity that would fain have blocked the Negro's advance have always been combatted valiantly and not without success by Southern whites.

The very Alabama that produced Tom-tom Heflin also produced, and in the same generation, Edgar Gardner Murphy. The same Georgia that is in socage to the Talmadges also tolerates Ralph McGill. "Our Bob" Reynolds flourished in North Carolina, but so did Howard W. Odum, and so do Frank P. Graham and Jonathan Daniels. If it can ever pay off its debt to the past, the South still has the germ plasm to produce great men, and they will be tempered and toughened by the tribulation through which they have come.

With the eyes of a child I once saw the process at work, although it was many years before I understood what I had seen. At the age of perhaps ten, I was one midsummer noon at the house of a kinsman when he came in to dinner from the cornfield where he had been stripping fodder, one of the nastiest jobs attached to farming in those days. This man had taken his degree at the University of North Carolina just in time to spend the ensuing four years as a trooper in Wheeler's Cavalry, C.S.A. But as he stepped up on the back porch that day there was nothing about him suggestive of either the scholar or the soldier. The oven heat of the cornfield had had sweat rolling off him all morning, and the black soil's powdery dust had settled and caked until he was inky except for his teeth and the whites of his eyes. On the shady porch I pumped, and he held his head and then his arms under the spout for a long time before it became evident that he was actually a white man.

But his comment on his own state has rung in my ears

ever since. When he had mopped his face and was toweling his hands and arms, he looked at me with a sardonic grin and broke into the thundering strophes of one of the *Georgics* of Vergil: *O fortunatos nimium, sua si bona norint, agricolas*—O most happy farmers, if only they knew their good fortune!

The small boy was merely startled by the rolling Latin measures, but an aging man knows now that he had there before his eyes the South triumphant. The soldier had returned from the war ruined, like everybody else. Like everybody else, he had moiled through thirty years of a depression that made the episode in Hoover's time a trifle by comparison. Not for his own fault, but by the ruin of his country, he had been sentenced to hard labor for the term of his natural life, with small hope of ever achieving ease, none of achieving luxury. Yet in the stifling heat of the cornfield, in a land of poverty and defeat, so far was he from broken that the ear of his mind could hear a great poet singing, and his stout heart could laugh at the absurdity of human fate.

The small boy gaped, but the aging man remembers how Desdemona found " 'twas strange . . . 'twas pitiful, 'twas wondrous pitiful. She wish'd she had not heard it . . . yet she wish'd that heaven had made her such a man." I, too, Desdemona, would to God I were such a man!

But he was my kinsman. However far I may fall short of his strength, we are of the same blood, of the same origin, we are of the South. Therefore, I would be ashamed to fall into despair because the rising generation in our land is hard put to it to cope with the same problem, unchanged except in the degree of its urgency. Time is running out, and the South must not only lift itself by its own bootstraps, but lift suddenly. The problem is what it has always been—to raise thirty per cent of the population, now handicapped, to the level of the rest, politically, economically, and culturally; the change is that it must be done more quickly than most of us had believed was imperatively necessary.

But to accomplish the feat, the white South must first lift itself to a moral and intellectual level higher than it has ever attained, or that has been attained by any dominant race anywhere in the world. It is a formidable task. It is so formidable that the Southern lower classes—lower, even though some have millions and pedigrees of enormous length —have shrunk back and renounced it. But the lower classes have always failed in every great emergency, so Faubus and Eastland and Talmadge are not of any large significance. The men who will count are the saving minority, unbroken and unbreakable, men who can respond to a challenge after the fashion of sturdy old Pierre-Samuel, the original Du Pont de Nemours. In 1816, when a swarm of troubles seemed about to overwhelm the new republic, he wrote to his old friend Jefferson: "We are but snails, and we have to climb the Andes. By God, we must climb!"

The South will climb. A romantic illusion? Possibly, but a living faith at this moment, nevertheless, and one not destroyed by reports from Little Rock, or even Poplarville, not shaken when presumably sane men talk of interposition, of concurrent majorities, of the compact theory of the Constitution. For it is precisely by wrestling and overthrowing the giants of madness and despair that the thews and sinews of the South will regain their old-time power, endowing it with the moral and intellectual vigor to become again the great instructor in political philosophy that it was when our history as a nation began.

I am a Southerner, and I wish the fact to be known; for the land of my birth is right now enduring the discipline that makes a nation great. So in the midst of its current tribulation, I can think of it as my toilworn kinsman did, and can echo his chant: *O fortunatos nimium*—O most happy land!

5

SCHOLIA ON GALBRAITH

In 1958, J. K. Galbraith, who had thitherto been regarded as an able but not particularly exciting professor of economics at Harvard, published a book that first startled and then stimulated large numbers of his fellow Americans. What shook up the laymen was the fact that it was an explanation that seemed to explain the national economy as it was operating in that year. Explanations we had had without number; but most of them were either statistical analyses of prevailing economic trends, factually accurate, no doubt, but socially insignificant; or if not that, then more or less thinly disguised propaganda for some panacea guaranteed to relieve all disturbances from cancer to ingrowing toenails. But *The Affluent Society* was different. Its merit was not in the therapy it suggested, but in the fact that it advanced a cause that, to the untutored mind, seemed as directly related to the national malaise as green apples are to the early summer bellyache of a ten-year-old boy.

Dr. Galbraith's thesis was promptly attacked at various points by various other economists. Since it is no part of the aim of this discourse to pass judgment on, or in any way to intervene in disputes among the faculty, no attempt will be made here to sustain the purely economic theories of the book. To the layman they seem, or most of them seem, to hold water; but that is a view that we sidewalk superintendents should accept tentatively. What we take to be incontestably true—and, in fact, it is not contested by any of the professional economists—is a dictum that falls clear of the field of economics. It is Galbraith's vigorous contention that the importance of the American standard of living is small by comparison with that of the American standard of life.

Now there is a point at which the bewildered American is not left behind at all, for the man who has not learned the difference between making a living and making a life has not learned much. Theories of value, monetary theories, the processing of statistics, the extrapolation of indexical data, and the calculus of exponential progressions may sink him, even when he has the help of Stuart Chase; but as between the terms "a living" and "a life," he is aware of a sharp distinction, even though he may have some difficulty in putting that distinction into words. So when he encounters an economist who appears to be alive to that difference, he is impressed, and no academic thunder, on the left or on the right, will remove the impression.

There is no mystery whatever in the dictum that one must make a living in order to have a chance to make a life, and none in the further statement that one may become so absorbed in the effort to make a living that he never finds time to live. Far from being discoveries of modern science, these are truisms familiar to every human being who is beyond the age of childhood and is capable of thought. But,

like many other things that everybody knows, their application to existing conditions is not always clear.

It is on this point that Galbraith, like Chapman, had the
wit—and perhaps the luck—to "speak out loud and bold,"
producing among laymen an effect that may have astonished
the author himself. It is not beyond belief that it may have
done more than astonish him—it may have disconcerted
him—for it is far from certain that the man intended to say
what, in effect, he did say. This is nothing uncommon, for
every writer whose book has rung a bell has, in the act of
striking the note he desired, produced overtones, harmonics
of astonishing variety. Charles Darwin, for example, certainly
never intended to say or to intimate that there is a definite
blood relationship between man and *Alouetta ursina,* the
howling monkey; but from what he did say the inference is
so extremely plausible as to be practically inescapable.
Whatever chimes with our experience, although it may have
been in strict truth merely suggested, is in effect said.

With this formal exoneration of the Harvard professor
entered on the record, it is legitimate to consider the effect
of *The Affluent Society* on the American who feels that the
scientific age has left him behind. The magnitude of that
effect is attested by the popularity of the book; but the
reasons for it are not measurable by statistics.

Superficially, the thing would seem to be as arrant a
defiance of common sense as that basic equation of quantum
theory, pq minus qp equals ih over $2pi,$ that is to say, equals
something other than zero. The impression the bewildered
layman first gets is that it is here asserted that the American
Miracle of Production is actually mere sleight of hand and
our apparently growing wealth is in fact increasing poverty.

The remarkable fact is that this is instantly understood by many who have not the faintest idea of what Max Planck had in mind. That is to say, we are aware of the fact, although not of its underlying reasons. We know that the common-sense view of our progress and prosperity is pretty fraudulent, but we do not know exactly why; the figures are there, and figures don't lie, but with every passing day we are more firmly convinced that some liar has certainly figured. We have been rolling in prosperity and it has done us no good at all, so any man who comes along with a rational explanation commands our instant and close attention.

Galbraith's view that not the currency alone but the whole economy is badly inflated is one that not many of us had thought through for ourselves, but once stated it is in essential agreement with common experience. The essence of inflation, as far as the ordinary man is concerned, is that the real value of things is less than it appears to be. As regards a dollar this is simple enough; but can the same thing be true of a desire? Some Americans can remember, and all have heard of, the runaway inflation that overwhelmed Germany after the First World War. In 1913 the sum of fifty thousand German marks represented nearly twelve thousand five hundred American dollars; but the time came when fifty thousand marks was the price of a postage stamp required to carry one letter from one post office to the next. This was inflation of the currency carried to the extreme.

When value disappears, wholly or partially, there is inflation. In 1960 it took a dollar and twenty-nine cents to buy what a dollar bought eleven years earlier. It is no strain

on the intellect to calculate that this represents an inflation
of twenty-nine per cent. So much for the currency.

But in 1960 there were a thousand things other than
money that were not worth as much as they were worth
eleven years earlier—a day off, for example. By 1960 the
five-day week had been pretty well established in industry,
commerce, and finance, and it is generally admitted that
two days of rest each week are better than one; but exactly
how much better is beyond mathematical calculation. Theoretically, two days should be twice as valuable as one, and to
some people they assuredly are, but not to everyone. Suspicion is widespread that to most people the satisfactions of
leisure are not multiplied by exactly the same figure as the
hours of leisure. The value per hour is somewhat reduced,
and a reduction of relative value is our definition of inflation.

Obviously, the means of checking this kind of inflation
cannot be devised by the Secretary of the Treasury, nor
by the Federal Reserve Board, who deal with money alone.
The value of a dollar may be reduced by circumstances
beyond the control of any individual, but the value of an
hour is determined by the man who spends it. He gets a
full sixty minutes' worth only if he does something with it
that in his own estimation is worth doing, sees, or hears,
or says something worth seeing, or hearing, or saying.

The qualification, "in his own estimation," is extremely
important, although many good people do not think so.
What a man thinks is worth while is what he wants; and
the satisfaction of a real want is all that justifies any expenditure, of money, of time, of energy, or of anything else.
Perhaps there are absolute standards of value, but no sage
as yet has been wise enough to define them except by the

vague term, satisfactions. There are some people who find genuine satisfaction in reading the poetry of Dylan Thomas, and some who find it in developing a powerful backhand stroke at tennis; yet there are those who consider neither of these worth two cents, two minutes, or the lifting of two fingers. All are right.

The subtle thief of value is the persuasion, of whatever form, that induces the tennis player to devote time to the poet, or the esthete to practice on the court, on the theory that a pretended interest in literature or sport is somehow meritorious. No pretense is meritorious.

All this was old stuff when The Preacher wrote "vanity of vanities, all is vanity," and that, according to the accepted computation, was something over two thousand nine hundred and thirty years ago; yet it is as modern as this morning's newspaper. It is certainly one source and may well be the primary source of the malaise of the American people in the latter half of the twentieth century. Furthermore, it is not within the purview of any specialist. In this matter the man who feels left behind is behind only verbally. He may be staggered by the terminology of contemporary theologians, psychiatrists, and manufacturers of tranquilizing drugs, but if by heroic effort he comes to understand them he may be taken aback to find that they throw the responsibility right on his own shoulders.

It is not always well to understand too clearly. Some years ago a learned doctor in the faculty of a Southern university developed an interest in collecting folk songs, especially the curious chants of labor gangs. He found two difficulties in his way: the direct approach usually provoked a shyness in the singers that halted the music; yet the odd rhythms and odder intonations of these products made them untelligible except through long and careful listening. So one day when he found a Negro street gang breaking up worn pavement with sledge hammers to the accompaniment of lusty singing, he seated himself on the campus wall and, while straining his ears, was careful to look another way, seeming to pay no attention. After a quarter of an hour he suddenly caught the meaning of the words and was rewarded in a singular way, for what the gang leader was singing as he wielded his hammer was:

> White man settin' on the wall (hanh!)
> White man settin' on the wall (hanh!)
> White man settin' on the wall all day,
> Wastin' his time,
> Wastin' his time!

To the extent that he is a mere status seeker, the man who feels left behind might as well be settin' on the wall all day, for he is assuredly wastin' his time. Most of us admit that, rationally, even when we have not apprehended it emotionally; but there are insidious forms of inflation that disturb the economists far more than the activities of blatant social climbers. For a man to spend his money, time, and energy on what he really wants to have or to do is psychologically sound and economically defensible, however it may horrify moralists. There is, to be sure, nothing to be said for activities that are physically or mentally destructive; heroin is not a good buy, even though the addict must have it. But no human being whose faculties are not in some way impaired really desires anything lethal.

The question is, Can our faculties be definitely impaired

although we are not addicts to alcohol, opium, hashish, or any of their derivatives? The belief is widespread, and Galbraith lends support to it, that the faculty of judgment, at least, not only can be but to a critical degree is impaired in millions of Americans who may never have taken a drink and would be appalled by the mere suggestion of smoking a reefer. They are weakened by the attacks of skillful creators of new desires, or pseudo-desires.

Impaired judgment is what leads a man to acquisition of things that he does not want. Impaired morals doubtless play a part, also, but from the point of view of this discussion not nearly so important a part as good people habitually assert. David Harum's remark that, as he surveyed his life, it was not the money he had spent for good times that he regretted, but the good times he might as well have had and didn't, is exactly to the point as far as it goes, but it doesn't go far enough. David should have regretted most of all the money he spent for good times that he didn't get.

The man—or at least the American—who feels left behind has only himself to blame when he goes where someone tells him a good time is to be had and finds it a very dull show. But will he admit it? Not once in a hundred times. As a rule he will not only say, but persuade himself really to believe, that what he is having is a good time; and whenever he does so he furthers the impairment of his own judgment.

This is well understood as it applies to seekers after culture who seek it according to a formula and not in response to an urge, but it gets less attention as it applies to those who are not seeking culture, or anything but diversion. The sturdy businessman drowsing through a symphony concert or an operatic performance to which he has been dragged by his wife has become one of the satirists' stock figures. But he is merely comic because he usually understands, if but dimly, the fraudulence of his course; the pathetic character is the man who endures boredom at the horse races when he might be having a fine time in a crap game. The pathos of it is that he honestly believes that he wanted to watch the nags rather than the galloping dominoes.

We commonly assume that no human being ever goes to the horse races unless he wants to go, but that assumption oversimplifies the conditions of modern existence. Our recreations, frivolities, and follies, no less than our labor and serious study, are affected by our notion of what is the thing to do, not what is most pleasant, and frequently suffer some diminution in value as a result.

Herbert Hoover, writing about the trip on which he accompanied President Harding to Alaska, confessed that on the outing he played so much bridge that he never liked the game afterward. In theory he was not compelled to play bridge or to do anything else. The trip had political overtones, with speeches to be delivered at various stops; but it was intended to be in the main a period of relaxation for the President and his close advisers, Mr. Hoover among them.

But Harding was the kind of man who could imagine no other form of amusement than bridge in a confined space, such as shipboard. He was also President of the United States, and if he wanted to play bridge, someone had to play with him. Thus Mr. Hoover incurred a permanent disability to enjoy a game that formerly he had found pleasant

enough, and he was the poorer for it. One of his diversions
had lost even more of its value than the 1960 dollar. Now
if a highly intelligent man can be forced by circumstances
into an impairment of his capacity for enjoyment, is there
much doubt that less vigorous minds are constantly being
trapped in similar fashion? Far less pressure than was
exerted on Mr. Hoover drives many a lesser man into forms
of amusement that do not amuse him at all.

From time immemorial moralists have bewailed the lavish
American expenditure on purchases that the moralists do not
approve. No doubt their lamentations are justified when the
nation spends upon wine, women, and song (as in the
colossal jazz records industry) far greater sums than are
spent on conversion of the heathen. But aside from the
moral quality of these indulgences there is the further
objection that they are so largely ineffective. Gambling in
any form is pretty generally accounted a vice; but surely it
is doubly vicious when a man does his betting at the pari-
mutuel window although he would much rather be rolling
the bones. It is sad that America is stupendously sinful, but
sadder still that so many of its sins are not the ones that it
really wants to commit.

Even in the combined sport and enterprise of patriotic
lying we have found ourselves handicapped by psychological
fetters that impede our efforts. Most observers are agreed
that our national propaganda was largely misdirected in the
fifteen years following the Second World War. We expended
much treasure and more effort informing the rest of the
world that we can afford to buy an infinity of gadgets that
are of very little value to any reasonable human being. We
played up the American standard of living to a yawning

world that might have been really interested in the American standard of life, whether high or low.

But by what foot rule can one measure that standard? By the home? By comparison with any other the typical American home is indeed a marvel of mechanical efficiency, but to what end? The obvious but inadequate answer is, to the end that the American housewife shall be relieved of drudgery. We resorted to mechanical ingenuity to supply the place of the almost vanished domestic servant. That may be accepted as proof of our mechanical ingenuity, but it may as logically be accepted as proof that we have made domestic service an intolerable way of life; which is not a point that makes good advertising copy.

Anyhow, why should the American housewife be relieved of drudgery? Presumptively in order that she may devote her time and energy to activities that yield greater satisfactions, certainly to her, and perhaps to society. This is a reputable explanation. To the extent that the housewife devotes her increased leisure to what is pleasurable and psychologically, if not financially, profitable to do, see, hear, or say, to that extent her husband's investment of hundreds, perhaps thousands, of dollars in housekeeping gadgets pays off, and is economically sound. But by the same token, to the extent that the leisure is invested in things that no woman in her right mind really wants, the expenditure is subjected to an inflationary deterioration.

Lest this discourse assume an intolerably pietistic tone, I hasten to record here a personal belief that the American woman has done moderately well in this respect. A strong, perhaps the strongest, bit of evidence to support this belief is the fact that she spends five hundred millions a year on beauty shops and twice as much more on cosmetics. This is the money investment, and it is probable that the time devoted to the purpose is an even larger percentage of a woman's total time than the money is of her total income.

It is time and money well spent. Many moralists and even some economists will deny this with heat; but the shocked are, if moralists, puritans, and if economists, Veblenites who accept uncritically old Thorstein's list of instances of conspicuous waste, although that list is largely idiotic. It is this writer's opinion that when any woman knows she is looking her best she speaks and acts more serenely, more amiably, and more intelligently than she does when she is gnawed by suspicion that she looks a fright. This is admittedly no more than an opinion, not susceptible of mathematical proof; but it is certainly not merely a man's opinion.

The woman void of all desire to enhance her personal attractiveness is so rare a specimen that she may be dismissed as negligible in any social survey; therefore, the time and money the typical woman devotes to that end are spent to satisfy a real want, with no pretense about it. They make a contribution to her happiness, and not hers alone. Most men, if they are honest about it, will admit that a profound insight into masculine psychology informs Mr. Ogden Nash's celebrated lines:

> A gal whose cheeks are daubed with paint
> Makes a hit with me over one whose ain't,

and when the gals make a hit the boys are happier. They may growl and grumble when the bills come in, but not many of them really disapprove the effort.

Of course reliance upon the beautician can be so ridiculously overdone as to defeat its own end. What human activity can't? But the real significance of the billions spent upon beauty aids is not that women are reckless wastrels, but that they know what they really want and go after it vigorously. It can be argued that in this respect they are getting more out of their increased leisure than American men are; and thus they suffer less from the inflation of the economy represented by the purchase of things that are not in fact desired.

The widely accepted theory of the cultural superiority of the American female leans heavily upon the preponderance of women in the audience at concerts, especially of symphonic and chamber music, at lectures, and in art museums. But this theory is suspect. It has some force, without doubt, but probably less than is generally attributed to it. The status seekers are not all male, perhaps not predominantly male. A woman attends a public event, not because she wants to go but, as often as a man, because she thinks it is the thing to do. Honegger bores as many American women as men, Klee perhaps more. To listen and to look without real pleasure is as fraudulent in one sex as in the other and, as touching the arts, perhaps as common.

But the pursuit of personal beauty by women is reality, and its formidable dimensions in the United States more than suggest that from the expanding economy women are deriving more genuine satisfactions than men. It does not follow that they are taking an unfair advantage of the situation. It is merely that they are more realistic, less easily deluded about what they really want, than men are. Brain washing, psychologists tell us, applied under sufficiently rigorous conditions, with sufficient persistence, over a sufficiently long time, can transform a bishop into a convinced atheist; but it is beyond imagination that equivalent pressure could ever persuade a woman that she really wants to look like an old bag, a traveling calamity causing all beholders to shudder and look aside.

So it appears that the man who feels left behind might be well advised to pay more attention to his womenfolk than to the scientists and inventors, the mathematicians and philosophers, who are advancing propositions and concepts before which his brain reels and his imagination boggles. It is a tenable supposition that these heavy thinkers are helling off in a direction in which the ordinary man is not going and has no desire to go. Let them pursue their own course.

But the women pose a different question. They show no marked disposition to sail off into outer space, physical or intellectual; so if they are getting ahead, getting more real value out of life, the American man not only feels, but in somber, solid fact he is, left behind. Who, then, is to blame? Not Planck and Einstein, not Teller and Oppenheimer, assuredly. Less certainly, but with high probability, not Kafka and Sartre, not Niebuhr and Tillich. Perhaps a little, but not very much, Madison Avenue and the mail-order houses. By far the larger share of the guilt lies upon none other than Benjamin Franklin Americanus who, before the Revolution, paid fivepence for a penny whistle, and who, since Eisenhower, pays five thousand dollars for a fin-tailed automobile that takes him there and brings him back no more efficiently and in view of the traffic jam, not much faster than did the Model T Tin Lizzie of fading memory.

It's ridiculous, but it's sinister, too. Barbara Ward noted recently the "loss of nerve and breakdown in confidence which occurs when societies have the impression that their ways are not the ways of the future—that history is leaving them behind." She finds only too much evidence that this is the present condition, not of the United States only, but of the Western world.

A loss of nerve and a breakdown in confidence are about as serious as anything that can happen to a man short of the Mikado's "something lingering, with boiling oil in it." Yet it is hard to deny that the much-touted Miracle of Production which has been the theme song of our propagandists for the past fifteen years has been accompanied by some loss of nerve and some breakdown in confidence— far from complete, but extensive enough to make a great many Americans awfully tired of hearing about that miracle.

Perhaps, though, it is actually a matter of grammatical tense. Perhaps we have not, like De Lawd in *Green Pastures*, passed a miracle, but have as yet only moved into position to pass one. The facilities for production are set up and in operation, but the economic goods that the machines turn out are no miracle—the machines can't do anything else. The miracle would be for all, or almost all, of the production to be converted into real values. The miracle would be a refutation, not by argument but in act, of Galbraith's complaint that a dangerously large proportion of the supposed values are phony.

One may indeed take the view, not without plausibility, that our present state is in itself a miracle, albeit of a backfiring, left-handed sort, of infernal, not celestial origin. When the American, endowed beyond all other men and beyond all precedent in his own history with wealth, with power, with ease and physical comfort, yet lives so hag-ridden by fears that

> Even such a man, so faint, so spiritless,
> So dull, so dead in look, so woebegone,
> Drew Priam's curtain in the dead of night,
> And would have told him half his Troy was burnt,

the situation is beyond a joke, beyond even a cosmic jest of sardonic gods. It is also something of a mystery. How do we do it? A candid examination of all media of publicity in 1960 showed nothing more striking than the pervasiveness of sounds of woe in every walk of life; and this during what was, in its every material aspect, one of the great years of our history. By what perverted chemistry can we, dowered to repletion with the honey of Hymettus, extract from it straight tincture of aloes?

The explanation, without doubt, is long, complex, and unedifying. More to the point than an attempt to analyze the process would seem to be an effort to determine to what extent it is reversible. Conviction of sin may be a necessary preliminary to repentance and reform, but it isn't either repentance or reform. Every pundit currently in active practice has, and has been volubly expounding, his own explanation of wherein the American people have gone wrong, and they are beginning to be a bore. A really persuasive formula for going right indubitably would startle and delight the country.

The technical procedures of the economists are not enough. We have had innumerable suggestions of that kind

—Galbraith supplies an elaborate one—but none has struck a spark, obviously because the blueprints must follow, not precede, the resolution to construct. It is conceivable, of course, that the feat is beyond our capacity; it may be that Norman Cousins' contention that modern man is obsolete has more truth in it than many of us are willing to admit; it may be that history has already left us hopelessly far behind.

Yet a doubt lingers. As a nation we are formally committed to the proposition that the pursuit of happiness is one of the inalienable rights of man; yet we know by experience that any right that is not constantly exercised tends to fade, to languish, eventually to fall into Cleveland's innocuous desuetude. If we have in fact failed to exercise vigorously and intelligently the right to the pursuit of happiness, it must have been slipping away from us, and the pallor, the languor of the modern temper is then and there explained.

But if that is the true explanation, our case is a long way from desperate. For to direct us toward the intelligent pursuit of happiness what is needed is not a super-Einstein, operating on the outermost fringes of thought, nor yet a secular Pentecost, miraculously opening our minds to the mysteries of modern science and setting us to conversing fluently in tongues unknown before. All we need is a Voice, like that of the Baptist crying in the wilderness—or perhaps not a Voice crying, but a translator reading in books of ancient wisdom and turning them into modern idiom.

Consider, for example, the world-old story of the time when they framed Socrates on a trumped-up charge, and Simmias, a practical businessman who knew how to meet a payroll, came whooping down from Thebes bringing with him a roll that would choke a cow. Simmias' intended procedure was practical and beautifully simple; he proposed to buy politicians on the hoof, not by the head but by the herd, and spring Socrates without bothering with courts and forms of law. What Socrates told him then about the intelligent pursuit of happiness, Plato heard and wrote down in matchless Greek. Centuries later, Jowett translated Plato into beautiful English. But who has translated Jowett into practical American? Who can?

Someone will, eventually. For there the inalienable right is defined with a precision never before and never since excelled by the wisdom of man. The trouble is that it applied to a specific situation that existed twenty-three centuries ago; and its significance will not be grasped by a majority of our people until it is applied in the language of today to the situation that exists today. But it is available, and the political leader who some day can and will announce it in the language of the radio and television audiences will produce an effect sensational beyond all computation. Furthermore, he will do much toward converting what is now legerdemain into a genuine Miracle of Production that will assure the prosperity and security of this country through more years than the living generation will be here to see.

6

THE PROPULSIVE STICK

ALL day long the noise of oratory had rolled through the reverberating Senate chamber, as one statesman after another discharged upon the palpitant air the bell tones of his immortal eloquence in a debate whose subject was long lost in oblivion. Nor is it worth seeking, for any subject will serve as an excuse for an oration by a Senator whose real purpose is not to persuade anyone, but to impress everyone with the extent of his understanding of what is wrong with the country. After many hours, as one Solon concluded a particularly impassioned description of the needs of the United States, a weary Vice President leaned to one side of his chair and muttered to a bystander, "What this country needs is a good five-cent cigar."

Thomas Riley Marshall, sometime Governor of Indiana, sometime Vice President of the United States, and always a most seemly gentleman, said there were two brothers, one of whom went to sea, while the other became Vice President —and neither was ever heard of again. But this applies, at most, to only twenty-five of the thirty-six men who have held the office. Death in the White House raised seven of them to the Presidency, three—Adams, Jefferson and Van Buren—were elected to that office, and the five-cent cigar has preserved Marshall's memory as it were in amber.

There are some who note this ruefully. Tom Marshall was a good man—honest, intelligent, liberal in his views, fair-minded, in all respects a fine type of public servant. To the serious-minded it seems unworthy that such a man should be remembered chiefly, if not entirely, for a jest.

But if regrettable frivolity is involved, yet it can be argued with some plausibility that it is not those who delight in the story who are less than serious-minded. For Marshall was not thinking about cigars alone. On his mind was the windy pomposity that all day long had excluded from the Senate chamber any intelligent discussion of matters of real moment, substituting for it empty gabble. Surely, to protest the waste of time in legislative halls is an endeavor of high seriousness; and whether to protest with a stiletto or with a blunderbuss would seem to be merely a matter of taste. Marshall disliked vain pretentiousness; and to be remembered for that is no meretricious fame.

However, Marshall flourished a long time ago, as is shown by the fact that he referred to a "five-cent" anything. It has been pointed out many times that the cigar the Vice President desired is still here, unchanged except that it now sells for fifteen cents; as if that were not a complete and utter change. Marshall sighed, not for tobacco, but for a stable value, which is perhaps the one adult wish as bootless as a baby's desire for the moon. "Riches take unto themselves wings," and even when they plod on leaden feet, still they move toward oblivion. Relentless deterioration in value is the one characteristic shared by every kind of money that the wit of man has invented.

But who believes this? Oh, we all accept it cerebrally, but not viscerally—rationally, but not emotionally. Most forms of money, paper currency for example, are vulnerable to the operations of tricksters in government and business, therefore are sure to be attacked and to suffer deterioration, soon or late. But that, we are likely to think, is because it was not sound money to begin with—not a genuine measure of value, such as gold. Yet a little reflection will show that the essential difference between Confederate currency and gold coin is that the Confederate dollar deteriorated faster and more completely than the gold dollar. At present the Treasury will pay for an ounce of gold thirty-five American dollars. At present the equivalent of one seventh of an ounce, that is to say, five dollars, in a first-class restaurant will buy a steak. In the time of Charlemagne it would have bought a steer. In the time of Alexander the Great, it would have bought a butcher. The deterioration of gold is slower, but not less certain than that of any other kind of money.

Marshall's joke therefore was, like most genuine humor, a wry comment on a tragic circumstance—the gulf that separates the aspiration of man from his achievement, the desire for stability and the accomplishment of flux. But the fact that the comment was wry is worthy of sharp attention as the hallmark of its Americanism. For assuredly it is, or it has been until recently, characteristic of Americans that, fully recognizing that the old gray mare, she ain't what she used to be, they testify to the fact with a comic ballad, not with a Book of Lamentations.

From Major Jack Downing and Sam Slick, through Artemus Ward, Mark Twain, and Martin Dooley, down as far as Will Rogers, the kind of American who became a popular idol has rarely wailed in the grip of relentless Destiny. He has jeered, always loudly, sometimes raucously; and in the jeering was great survival value. So at least it seems to the man who feels left behind when he takes note of the all but universal praise of the "well-adjusted personality," and the all but universal condemnation of the noisy Nay-sayer in the period following the Second World War. If we have lost something of great survival value our total national defense is weakened by just that much, and any reduction in the strength of our defense is no joke.

Of course this argument makes little impression on those who regard the psychological factor as of minor importance in the Cold War against communism. If the military factor overshadows everything else, then our military defenses alone are worth serious consideration. But the accuracy of that view turns upon the identity of our enemy. If we are fighting Russia, then our logical course is to stand to our arms, for the Russians are tangible, visible objects, suitable targets for gunfire; but if we are fighting communism, then we must adapt our weapons to the nature of the foe. Communism is not a suitable target for gunfire. As lead is considered no good against a witch who can be slain only with a silver bullet, so an idea can be shot down only with another idea, and in an ideological war the side that first runs short of ideas is in danger of losing.

In 1960 the Red army was standing exactly where it

stood fifteen years earlier except for a few small areas—
Austria, for example—that it had evacuated for reasons of
its own. But to suggest that communism made no advance
between 1945 and 1960 would be preposterous. It had
advanced so far as to make our situation uncomfortable,
not to say critical, and it had made its gains by the use of
psychological weapons. Obviously, then, our psychological
defenses have been dangerously ineffective and are in need
of very close attention.

A psychological weapon that the Russians have employed
with spectacular success is that manipulation of the con-
ditioned reflex popularly called "brain washing." It would
seem, then, that anything known to be an effective defense
against brain washing is an item of armament that should
be greatly valued by our side. But psychologists who have
made intensive studies of the process are pretty well agreed
that the subject most difficult to brain wash is one with a
sense of humor; and genuine humor does not exist in the
absence of a profound sense of the tragic. The absurdity of
man's fate is, after all, the cosmic jest from which all others
derive.

But a solemn ass has no sense of the tragic. The lugubrious
marks the limit of his understanding. Thus he is as vulnerable to brain washing as any subject in the world; he can,
and he does, suffer it without being subjected to any of the
physical rigors applied to prisoners of the Communists. He
can be brain washed without ever leaving the territory of
the United States and by nothing more rigorous than the
baying of the Communist hounds. Consider those Americans
who have been most conspicuously insistent upon our
adopting the methods of communism, instead of relying on

time-tested Americanism in the Cold War. Almost without exception they are dull dogs, capable, perhaps, of Goldsmith's "loud laugh that spoke the vacant mind," but as incapable of a bitter smile as they are of piling Pelion upon Ossa. Such men are gaps in our defenses, and there is all too much evidence to indicate that if they have not multiplied in recent years, they have certainly invaded high places in ominous numbers.

This is one sense and perhaps *the* one sense in which the man who feels left behind has no desire to catch up, for loss of any effective defense against Communist ideology is not progress.

Loss of the sense of humor means loss of appreciation of the fine distinction between contempt and hate, and is a loss indeed because it impairs ability to build up the kind of public opinion that is most resistant to the mass hysteria that culminates in mass idiocy. The distinction is a fine one, without doubt. In the range of the emotions contempt and hate would seem to be adjacent; yet for generations the ordinary American was able to distinguish between them. When Whitman spoke of "the audacity of elected persons"; when Artemus Ward remarked, "I am not a politician, and my other habits are good"; when Mark Twain began a lecture with, "Suppose you were a Congressman. And suppose you were an idiot—but I repeat myself"—in none of these cases did the contemporary generation fall into the delusion that the satirists really hated politicians. Oh, no doubt there were a few humorless individuals who were shocked, but in the main the audience understood perfectly, because in the main it shared the attitude of good-humored contempt that the utterances expressed.

But do Americans understand that attitude today? It is hard to believe, as one observes current performances in Congress and state legislatures, on the rostrum, in the newspapers, and even, occasionally, in the pulpit. It seems to be the fashion to take any expression of mild disgust as evidence of venomous hatred. Any dissent is equated with an attempt at subversion. It is not enough to abstain from disloyal conduct; one must swear to one's loyalty with resounding oaths.

The cult of the superior man is obviously far gone in decay. Time was when a long and honorable career, especially in public life, was accepted as proof of a man's membership in that "natural aristocracy" of which Jefferson wrote to John Adams; and the conduct of the natural aristocrat set the standard of honor. But the modern trend is to deny the existence of the superior man and to assume that we all lack only the opportunity to indulge in conduct as rascally as that of the worst offscourings of society. So the standard of honor is set by the audacity of Whitman's elected persons, the habits of Artemus Ward's politicians, and the intelligence of Mark Twain's idiot Congressman.

This annoys the intelligent, but it does much worse—it destroys the informed, but unintelligent. Pope's rhetorical question, "Who breaks a butterfly upon a wheel?" now has a most prosaic, literal answer—the UnAmerican Activities Committees. I use the term generically to include not only the committees set up by Congress, but also those set up by state legislatures and other agencies whose ukases have

the force of law. The record of these committees in dealing
with men of genius is appalling, but it is a minor offense
by comparison with what they have done to relatively
obscure individuals whose real trouble was merely carrying
a deck load of education that had sunk them beyond the
Plimsoll line drawn by their experience and judgment.
The men of genius survived, for the most part, and some
of them actually profited intellectually and morally, if not
financially, by the ordeal. But the poor devils whose intellectual soil had been exhausted by overcultivation were
done for permanently.

Many of them, perhaps most of them, were guilty as
charged; but the charge was, in the last analysis, the one
that was brought against the witches of Salem—contuma-
cious disregard of popular prejudice. He who is not guilty
of that charge is a second-rate—or a third- or fourth-rate
—character, therefore not a first-rate citizen. But there is
worldly wisdom in the selection of ways to register that
disregard. The man who stands in the path of stampeding
Gadarine swine lacks judgment, although you must allow
him credit for courage; and it was precisely for this one
admirable quality that many of these people suffered.

In this connection it is probable that few Americans
possessed of decent instincts have come through without
at least one sore spot that no kind of sophistical liniment
can assuage. In my own city at the height of the orgies I
was appealed to by a young woman caught under the car
of Juggernaut. She was a member of a good family, well
brought up, a college graduate, and endowed with a lively,
if not powerful, intelligence. She looked it all—no can-

didate for Miss America, but definitely easy on the eyes,
well turned out because she knew not only how to choose
her clothes, but also how to wear them.

I could do nothing for her because she was guilty—not
of espionage, for she knew no secrets, not of perjury, for
she was no government employee and had taken no oath,
not of treasonably adhering to the enemies of the United
States, for at the time the United States had no enemies
within the meaning of the law. But in instructing a class in
various theories of radicalism—in itself legitimate—she had
used unauthorized textbooks that advocated in principle
the overthrow of the government by force and violence.

Had she stuck to the canonical texts the catchpolls could
not have laid a finger on her—such subversive documents
as, for example, *Common Sense* by Thomas Paine, the
Declaration of American Independence by Thomas Jefferson,
and the *Speech to the Virginia Convention* by Patrick Henry.
All these not only advocated but actually excited force and
violence leading to the overthrow of the government.

Instead, she chose certain relatively gaseous and ineffective utterances that had produced no immediate results,
such as the writings of Marx and Engels. To these she may
have added some of the arguments of Lenin but these, of
course, were designed not to overthrow, but to strengthen
the state. However, under the law of the United States and
the State of Maryland, as the law then stood, it was a crime
to teach children any argument for the overthrow of government except an argument of demonstrated potency to produce an overthrow. The arguments this woman used had
proved futile in the past, so she was convicted and sentenced

to three years in prison. As I see it, she went to jail, not for endangering the state, but for failing to endanger it.

But she went to jail. Four years later, while waiting for a train in the crowded Pennsylvania station in New York, I spied a vacant seat and occupied it without glancing to right or left. Then a woman at my elbow called me by name, and I looked around into the face of a stranger, a ravaged face above the body of a charwoman. It was what three years in prison had done to the woman whom I had been unable to help.

We chatted vaguely for a few minutes. I did not mention the word "prison" and neither did she. Presently I made an excuse and fled, shaken, and leaving, I am certain, a woman who thinks I was ashamed to be seen talking to her. I was ashamed, all right, bitterly ashamed, but not of being seen. I was ashamed to look her in the face. As a citizen of a self-governing state I am in some measure responsible for what my government does; and what it had done to this woman it did, ostensibly, in order that I may sleep well o' nights. Four years earlier, when she passed, loitering oafs would have said, "What a dish!" Today they would say, "What a bag!" To do that to a woman is a crime compared to which simple murder is almost benevolent; and the reflection that it was done to assure my safety filled one free-born American citizen with all the pride of a whipped cur.

Certainly it was largely my fault. A man of real courage cannot be thrown off balance by a sudden confrontation. There was a flaw in Lord Jim, or he wouldn't have jumped when the ship seemed certain to go down; but the scarred man's consciousness of his own guilt did nothing to reduce his bitter contempt for those who put him in the false position. Nor does realization that in a sudden emergency I acted like a heel mollify my resentment for those responsible for creating the emergency—the hysterical mobs in Congress and in state legislatures who have enacted laws based on the intelligence of Simple Simon and the justice of Ivan the Terrible. They got me into the mess, and that I don't forget.

The protest against this sort of thing has been vigorous and, among the intelligent, almost unanimous; but to date it has been strangely ineffective. Perhaps its futility is due in part to its being too exclusively intelligent, and in practical politics intelligence is not enough. A certain measure of raucousness is also needed. None will deny that John Hay, Theodore Roosevelt's first Secretary of State, was an intelligent man; yet Hay is usually identified as the unnamed official who told Henry Adams that the only effective way to deal with a Congressman is to take a stick and hit him on the snout.

Surely no rational man believes that Hay applied that to each and every member of the House of Representatives, which at the time included a number of men who were at least equal to John Hay in intellect and character; but he did apply it to enough to give the statement some color of verity. Quoth David the King, "I said in my haste, All men are liars." The phrase "in my haste" certainly implies some error; yet David at leisure did not retract the statement. Evidently he held it to be as sound as most generalities.

Asininity does intrude into the conduct of public affairs

in this as in other countries. No one with the slightest touch of realism in his make-up will deny that, for all recorded history attests it. But Americans in recent years have developed a curious allergy to any forthright identification of the asinine. All comment must be as they say temperate, by which they mean tepid. Even the downright wicked must be labeled as such more in sorrow than in anger, for while the Dishonorable Mr. X is indubitably a crook, it is to be assumed that he is the victim of an unfortunate environment and probably the product of a broken home. But it is utterly beyond the pale to state truly that the technically Honorable Mr. Y, while honest enough if it is a matter of stealing your watch, is nevertheless an arrant jackass, playing more hell in more ways than Boss Tweed and his whole camorra ever dreamed of. Why? The most superficial acquaintance with political history, here or in any other country, is enough to show that impeccably righteous fools in high office have done more damage to the world than the massed battalions of the villains. What is the basis of the inhibition upon noting the fact and citing modern instances?

Presumably war psychology has something to do with it. Since war is an encourager of two virtues only, courage and endurance, and is otherwise the summation of all vices, falsehood and fraud are integral parts of it. Whether or not unity exists, the appearance of national unity is imperatively necessary when we are facing an armed enemy. Twice within the memory of men and women who are not yet old we have been engaged in desperate military conflict, when political criticism could not be tolerated; and it is fatally easy for men to regard what circumstances make necessary as *per se* right and proper. This delusion is perhaps the reagent that has attacked and partially dissolved not only freedom of speech, but even the American sense of reality.

All mentally alert Americans are aware of the corrosion of liberty and many of them have commented on it, but usually in a mood of detachment not warranted by the facts. It is the fashion to ascribe our malaises to usurpation of the seats of power by the senseless. Seldom is it explained as an abdication by the sensible. It is not, in fact, a total abdication, rather an abandonment of one of the two functions that fate assigns to the thoughtful in the process of social development.

We have long accepted the picture of the mass of mankind as the donkey, lured on by the carrot held in front of his nose, and at the same time urged on by the stick smartly applied to his hindquarters; and we agree that men of sense have the double duty of holding out the carrot and wielding the stick. But, consciously or unconsciously, we habitually restrict the picture to the mass, the unthinking, the *mobile vulgus*. We are reluctant to admit, and ordinarily we vehemently deny, that the intellectual is precisely the same kind of donkey, moving briskly only when the lure of the carrot is reinforced by the sting of the stick. The fact that his proper response is rapid thought, rather than rapid action, is immaterial.

Nor should it be necessary to labor the point that while the essential nature of the brute is common to the whole species, there are wide variations in the thickness of the hide of individual specimens; hence the choice of the appropriate stick calls for nice judgment. Some are obsolete, others losing effectiveness. Fear of Jonathan Edwards' type of hell can raise weals on few literate Americans today, and fear of what Baltimoreans call the espantoon of the cop on the beat is not much more effective. Fear of the atomic bomb and its successor still counts, but for much less than fear of various intangibles—communism, subversion, alien ideologies, "all them foreign *isms*."

But for the intelligent intellectual (that is, sad to say, not a tautology) none of these goads stings with half the sharpness of the fear of being exposed as a hollow and pretentious fellow. It haunts him because he knows how easily it can be done. Any man who is half-, nay, quarter-educated must be keenly aware of how little he really knows; and if he suspects the presence of some archer lurking in the bush with a quiverful of barbed criticisms, he is wary of presenting a target.

It is for that reason more than any other that I lament the absence of the most accurate bowman of the twentieth century, the late H. L. Mencken. Popular mythology has it that Mencken was the scourge of the boobs, although the fact is that he rejoiced in genuine boobs and held them in warm affection. His shafts were not aimed at them, but at pseudo-intellectuals, and at real intellectuals when they diverged from the straight and narrow path of reason.

None of Mencken's darts ever penetrated anything solid, but the havoc he wreaked upon inflated balloons made him the terror of the age, and this salutary fear constituted much of his value to his generation. In fact, I am persuaded that the vast execution that he worked upon pomposities was the minor part of his service to society; the major part, and by long odds, was the vaster number of pomposities he prevented from appearing.

For no man who walks in shoe leather is wise at all times. Homer nods and, being human, he will nod the more frequently when there is no penalty for being caught napping. The twang of Mencken's bowstring usually meant the irremedial puncture of one stuffed shirt. So much is common knowledge. What is generally overlooked is that at the same moment it threw the fear of damnation into the breasts of a dozen men who might have been on the verge of speaking without thinking, causing them to pause and perhaps rearrange their ideas to the salvation of their reputations. This, I submit, was twelve times as important a public service as the flattening of one blown-up bladder.

Mencken and I disagreed fundamentally, but as we were in perfect accord on trivialities our encounters were always amicable. I thought, and still think, his philosophy unsound and his politics fantastic; he, I have no doubt, regarded me as philosophically ignorant and politically idiotic. But what of it? Perhaps we were both right. At any rate, the incontestable truth is that a healthy fear of the flick of his lash restrained me from committing even more follies than I did commit. Nothing will shake my belief that he had the same effect on many others, with the result that the sum total of imbecility in American life and letters was substantially reduced by his presence among us. There are doubtless greater services that an individual can render to his time. But not many.

However, we have left Mencken behind, and I am stubbornly unconvinced that that is progress. On the contrary,

I believe it is retrogression, doubly deplorable because of its timing. A period in which pressure of events is forcing a wholesale revaluation of values, a widespread shift of attitudes as well as ideas, is obviously a period in which great mistakes are not merely possible, but virtually inevitable. To hold such mistakes to the irreducible minimum should be our chief concern. To this end every new idea advanced should be subjected to every imaginable test, including the acid test of scorn. All other tests we seem to be applying vigorously, but for scorn we have for the most part substituted mere denigration which, like many another substitute, is very nearly worthless. For genuine scorn implies understanding; it cannot, as calumny can, be the product of an empty mind.

Above all, we are lavish with moral indignation. I am in disagreement with Mencken as to the utility of that emotion. I consider it an excellent implement in skilled hands, but, like any other fine tool, it loses most of its efficacy when manipulated clumsily.

Here enters the necessity for that nice discrimination, mentioned earlier, between contempt and hate. Contempt has as its basis an appreciation of the excellent; no such restriction applies to hate. But appreciation of the excellent is the hallmark of the superior man; and the poison in that perversion of democracy that people call leveling and pedants call egalitarianism is its repudiation of the concept of the superior man. Historically, it has its justification, of course, in that the prerogative of superiority has frequently been appropriated by people who were not superior. Mankind, taught by experience that the aristocracies of the past have been based on Jefferson's "virtue and talents" less often than on the prehensile aptitude of their members, has much reason, if no valid excuse, for denying the existence of the *aristoi*.

But it comes close to being an excuse when the *aristoi* make no effort to claim their own prerogative, and tacitly acquiesce in the activities of the levelers. One of the most vicious of these is the disposition, apparently increasing, to attach moral turpitude to controversy. The really fanatical levelers make it absolute. The more moderate are willing, at least in theory, to tolerate dissent provided it is ostensibly aimed at the substitution of a better idea, rather than merely at the destruction of a bad one. What they call "constructive criticism" is permissible, although they view it somewhat as bachelor St. Paul viewed marriage—as an unfortunate necessity.

Under no circumstances, however, may criticism be offered except with the mournful decorum of the undertaker's assistants at a high-toned funeral. And this invalidates it to some extent, usually to a large extent, because it removes most of the sting, and it is the sting that propels the donkey. Consider the unguent that most of the respectable mingled with their scanty criticism of the late Joseph McCarthy when he was at the height of his catastrophic career: "I thoroughly approve his purpose although I cannot accept his methods." They meant his avowed purpose, which was not necessarily his real one. But the highest and holiest purpose cannot make a dirty deed anything but dirty. McCarthy's avowed purpose was the elimination of Communist influence from government; but if it had been much more elevated, if his real purpose had been, say, nothing less than to embed the Shorter Catechism in the mind of every infant Turk, still his methods would have been every whit as calamitous and disgraceful.

On Memorial Day, 1960, Leo Szilard, having been informed by his doctors that he had at most only a few months to live, addressed to the American people a statement to which they should give the serious consideration by law accorded to a dying declaration. He warned us not to lay upon politicians alone blame for the failure during the previous eight years to advance a single step toward establishment of a just and lasting peace. He asserted that it was a failure of intellectual leadership, all of it, in this nation.

Such a statement from such a man cannot be dismissed with a shrug. Even if we believe that the failure is more apparent than real, it behooves us to investigate sedulously the reasons for this appearance of failure. The hasty and forthright will explain it with a single word—cowardice. But that simply raises another question, to wit, Of what are intelligent intellectuals afraid? The guillotine? In the first place, it is outmoded; of the hundreds of victims of the emotional orgy known as McCarthyism two wretches only were actually sent to join the Salem witches; and in the second place, if intellectual integrity is no longer backed by physical courage, talk of the future of the republic is wasted breath.

It is easier to believe that not cowardice but resentment is the impediment that handicaps our natural aristocracy; which would mean that it is not fully aristocratic. With virtue and with talents, but lacking full appreciation that *noblesse oblige,* it remains a bit plebeian. "Gentlemen," a sardonic professor of English taught my class when the century was young, "the most profitless form of endeavor open to man is that of skinning a jackass; for you may rest assured that the jackass will never thank you, and nobody else gives a damn." He had in mind the practice of literary criticism, but the relevance of his words to political activity is plain.

It is nonetheless a repudiation of the aristocratic attitude toward public service. Effort without reward or hope of reward is the recognized obligation of the classes that really are upper in more than pride and privilege. Americans already recognize that as regards monetary reward; not scholars and scientists only, but businessmen, frankly avowing the profit motive in ordinary transactions, admit that it is their duty to work for a dollar a year when the country really needs their services.

But most of us still feel that a conspicuous contribution to the general welfare does entitle a man to the respectful consideration of his fellow citizens. In principle it does. Nevertheless, failure to collect any reward, not even common politeness, relieves no man of the obligation to perform the service.

If his particular talent happens to be that of an adept and efficient skinner of jackasses, he must skin 'em, undeterred by his failure to receive thanks. Profitless though it may be, it is public service; for the jackass properly skinned ceases to bray, and therefore will not stimulate every other ass in the drove to lift his voice in a cacophony that will deafen the ears of the nation to the urgings of common sense and common decency.

7

THE VANISHING STATE
OF MIND

THE late Senator Broughton, of North Carolina, used to repeat with delight a story from World War I, when the American Thirtieth Division, recruited largely in the Carolinas and brigaded with the British, was fighting across Belgian terrain that four years of war had churned into a semiliquid loblolly. In a heavy raid on one of our outposts a hundred Germans piled into what passed for trenches and at the height of the melée that ensued some inspired genius of an artilleryman—maybe German, maybe American —slung a six-inch high-explosive shell into the middle of the mess, hoisting the slop to engulf friend and foe alike.

A rescue party with shovels dashed up and exhumed objects unidentifiable, but gasping and choking and more or less alive. The lieutenant in command, desperately trying to straighten things out, yelled at one such object, "Who are you?"

"Glub-glub," replied the object, spitting out a mouthful of mud.

"Who are you?" shouted the officer again. "Are you an American?"

"N-no, sir," was the answer. "I'm from Harnett County."

Far be it from me to asperse the fair name of Harnett, a noble county if it had done no more than ornament North Carolina with Paul Green, dramatist, essayist, novelist, and perhaps the greatest pageant master in America; but this happened long ago, when Harnett was rural, remote and unsophisticated, so ribald Tarheels fell upon the story with glee. But their derision perhaps was misapplied. The soldier's answer may have branded him as naïve, but it may just as logically be taken as evidence of an autochthony that has since been disappearing from American life, not necessarily to its improvement. That man was from Harnett first, from North Carolina second, and from America third; nevertheless, one who held the line when the Germans were swarming in and the big shells were exploding, was American enough for all practical purposes. It is my belief, furthermore, that in Belgium he fought well for America precisely because in North Carolina he would have fought stupendously for Harnett.

But we are leaving all that behind. Who is from Harnett, who today is from any one spot in this continental domain? Boston, they said in the nineteenth century, is not a place, it is a state of mind. On Boston I am no authority, but I am sure that as recently as thirty years ago it was true of the ancient and comparatively honorable city of Baltimore, with which I am better acquainted. But that the state of mind persists I am not at all sure. At the Patuxent River, twelve miles northeast of the District of Columbia line, a city begins and it straggles all the way to Havre de Grace, on the Susquehanna, sixty-odd miles away. Somewhere in this

nebulosity is, or was, Baltimore, but its geographical limits
are vague, and it is less a state of mind than a faint, sub-
liminal urge.

To be sure, the statutes decree that certain lines run by
surveyors and located by geodetic coördinates shall be considered the city limits of Baltimore; but no rational human
being does so consider them. Tax authorities and court
officials, yes; but such functionaries when acting in their
official capacity are hardly to be regarded as rational human
beings.

From the public prints I gather that as much may be said
of all the country's dozen biggest cities, and to some extent
is true of many smaller ones. It may be plausibly argued,
indeed, that the area delimited by the legal boundaries is
precisely not the city of Baltimore, merely the spot where it
once was, but whence it has vanished.

Consider this: in the census of 1960 Baltimore proper lost
26,000 population, while Baltimore improper, technically
known as the metropolitan district, gained 400,000. A fact
not shown in the preliminary reports, but which may show
up in the detailed census findings, is that the great bulk
of the increase in the suburbs was drawn from the central
city, and that this loss was partially made good by immi-
gration from a distance. That is to say, the city lost, roughly,
400,000 Baltimoreans and received about 375,000 people
who cannot be so designated.

A state of mind is not, generally speaking, an overnight
creation. It takes time to make a genuine urbanite, and in
the older cities it takes a long time.

"No," said an old lady of Baltimore's Mount Royal section

in response to a question about another woman, "I wouldn't call her a member of one of the *old* families. Her people moved here some years *after* the War of 1812."

The old lady's standard is doubtless a bit extreme but there is no doubt that the 1960 population includes some hundreds of thousands of people who are not yet Baltimoreans by any standard more rigorous than that of the law establishing voting residence. They are, in Daisy Ashford's phrase, "mere people," and while it is a reasonable expectation that in time they will—to quote Miss Ashford again—"become less mere," that time is not yet; and it is the existing condition of the city that engages the interest of social workers, budget directors, and the police.

Yet current discussion of the problems of the American city, omnipresent in the reviews, the journals of opinion, and the news magazines and papers, slides around certain aspects of it, presumably because frank discussion might offend certain sensibilities, and public discussion must under no circumstances offend anybody. But if there is a single mathematical certainty in this world, it is certain that you cannot solve any problem correctly without giving due weight to all the factors involved, not to a selected few.

For instance, it is seldom considered necessary to defend the existence of the city on psychological grounds, although a vigorous defense is clearly needed. No big city is physically fit for human habitation. The noise, the crowding, the atmospheric pollution, and the inconvenience are such as sentient beings should not be called on to endure save for compelling reasons. Only as the city offers psychic benefits to counterbalance its physical hardships does it become tolerable and even attractive as a place of residence; and American cities are steadily losing the capacity to offer such benefits.

In the old days two apparently opposite human impulses, the gregarious instinct and the desire for privacy, worked together to overcome the city's disadvantages. In a large city the oddest human types can enjoy the society of their kind with relatively little difficulty; and at the same time a large city makes possible an anonymity that is a passable substitute for privacy. These, combined, still constitute a cohesive power of great magnitude, but not great enough to resist the centrifugal forces of modern times. Gregariousness and privacy must be supplemented if the American city is to survive as a city, and not as a sort of concentration camp *de luxe*.

This effect of modern technology is not, of course, confined to the city. At the time of World War I, large areas of Harnett County still had the powerful attraction of unspoiled nature, an attraction that has been rapidly disappearing since.

Against it, at the time of World War I, Baltimore still had the attraction of the *polis*, with the meaning that the Greeks attached to that term—the center of cultural and political as well as of economic activity. It, too, has been losing its attraction steadily.

Not much is said of this by gentlemanly modern critics because of the implied slur upon the rube, the bumpkin, the hayseed. But why not slur him? He deserves it. Certainly the countryman has characteristic virtues, but his characteristic vices are quite as objectionable as those of his opposite number, the city punk. The point, though, is not an estimate of the relative value of the two modes of life, but their equal loss of value, or at least of their grip upon the imaginations and emotions of men. In the event of a third World War, God forbid!, would an unrecognizable soldier, asked to identify himself, reply instinctively that he was from Harnett County, or from Baltimore City? Some might, but their number decreases; and into the chorus of rejoicing over this decrease of parochialism it is my deliberate intent to inject a sour note.

It is justifiable for, if we are to adopt a reasonable course in any situation, it is essential to consider every element in that situation, including those that may be regrettable. Naturally, this applies to the older generation. Americans who were boys or girls of ten at the end of the Second World War are exempt, for they have no experience of the old ways of life, and cannot fairly be held responsible for carrying over its virtues, if any, into the new environment.

But as far as the older generation is concerned, it is not merely advisable, it is imperatively necessary to think as fast as Captain Flagg in *What Price Glory?* For if the older generation is to retain status at all, it must offer the younger a sufficient excuse for its continued existence. Complacent elders tend to flatter themselves that what they have done in the past entitles them to consideration and respect during the latter part of their lives, and it may once have been true; but if what the senior generation has done in the past has been largely swept away, the claim is largely swept away, too. As regards the American city, that is the case. The reasons for preferring urban life have been so far invalidated by a combination of stupidity and greed that the

cities are dying; and there is no compelling reason for according respect and consideration to the generation that let
them die.

It is incumbent upon the oldsters, then, to establish other
reasons for tolerating their continued existence, and the one
practical method by which it may be done is by exhibiting
a superior understanding of the world in which we all live.
Age of itself confers no rights. Age of itself is an offense.
The Struldbrugs, in *Gulliver's Travels,* were a race of im-
mortals but the most miserable of all creatures, and the birth
of one was regarded as a presage of national calamity. But
the offense of being old may be palliated, and even over-
compensated. Agamemnon wished he had ten men like
Nestor, not like Ajax. But the overcompensation is effected
by conscious effort, not by native charm. It is true that there
are handsome old people, but not many; the vast majority
cannot be considered adornments of the landscape. And if
it is true that there are many valuable old people, it is not
by virtue of their being old, but because they have been
able to extract social value from their experience.

Hence the American, especially the city dweller, who has
reached or is approaching middle age is nearing the time
when his justification for continuing to cumber the ground
will be progressively less evident unless he bestirs himself
to make it so. He is not in the happy position of his grandfather, or even of his father. He cannot point to a splendid
creation and say, "My work." Rather, he resembles an anti-
Augustus who found Rome marble and left it brick, seeing
that during the period of his dominance the cities have been
steadily degenerating into slums—a progression unchecked

except in a relatively few spots where the more noisome slums have been demolished and replaced by barracks into which the hopelessly inefficient and irresponsible elements of the population are herded. There is real danger that the people who have been in control of American cities from the end of the Second World War may go down in history as the most worthless generation since the foundation of the republic.

For it is in this period that the city attained an overwhelmingly dominant position in American life. We had seen it coming. The trend had been continuous for fifty years, but the great rush came after the Second World War. Our generation was not prepared to handle it. We didn't try to handle it. We took to our heels, fatuously believing that we could outrun the flood, with the result that the rising generation must perform Herculean labor to avoid going under. For the appalling aggregations of population, especially along the northern Atlantic seaboard, are not cities in any accepted meaning of the term, are not American in any sense except geographically, and are not viable in their present amorphous condition. Without a vastly improved social and political organization they are bound to become colossal death traps, even if the Russians—and the Albanians and the Bulgarians and all other nations—refrain from dropping a single hydrogen bomb upon them.

The organization will no doubt be effected by the next generation, but at an immensely greater cost, social and political as well as monetary, than would have been necessary had this generation done its duty instead of expending its ingenuity in evasion and avoidance. For the building of a city worthy of the name involves great labor and great cost, and our generation has evinced little disposition either to work or to pay.

For a city worthy of the name is not a combination of land, houses, and people. A concentration camp or an army cantonment has all three, but it is not a city; the true *polis* is in fact a state of mind, and if it becomes a metropolis, a mother city, it is merely an intensified state of mind. It is the conviction that life can be made richer, more beautiful, more intense, in literal truth more abundant, when great numbers of men act together to make it so. Periclean Athens, Medicean Florence, even Augustan Rome could have been swallowed whole by modern Baltimore; but if you want to contend that Baltimore is therefore a greater city, go ahead, but I must respectfully decline to follow.

The mere physical doom of the Boston-to-Baltimore aggregation, of the southern California complex, and of others except, perhaps, the one along the Great Lakes, as they are now organized, can be pronounced in the one word, water. New York and Philadelphia are already in competition for the water of the Delaware, Philadelphia and Baltimore for that of the Susquehanna, and all New England is squabbling over every rivulet. The obvious answer is the Atlantic ocean, but the demineralization of sea water is at present so appallingly expensive as to be out of the question, and not until 1945 was there even a hint that it would ever be otherwise.

In that year the development of atomic fission on a massive scale, with the attendant generation of enormous heat, did supply a hint, but it has not been followed up for the reason that the energy and expense of the necessary

research are beyond the means of the invidiual cities, even
of New York. In combination they might have managed it,
but how were they to combine? It is impossible without
a radically different political organization.

It is highly probable, however, that long before the question of water supply becomes acute Megalopolis will come
to grief through the breakdown of other indispensable services, not all, and not the most important of them, physical.
But the physical are threatening enough. Transportation is
already dreadfully, if not hopelessly, snarled, police and fire
protection grow steadily more difficult and more expensive,
and educational and recreational facilities, despite frantic
building, are less and less adequate.

Still, these are all technological problems, not beyond the
competence of engineers, architects, and financiers. What is
far more sinister in the eyes of a man left behind with old-
fashioned notions of citizenship is an apparent repudiation
of responsibility by our American equivalent of the nobility
and gentry of monarchical government. The calamity of the
American city is less the influx of bums than the fact that
the gentlemen have run out.

Suburbia is regarded as, and until quite recently has been,
Margaret Halsey dissenting, a highly desirable place of residence. Nevertheless, it constitutes a malignant growth
sapping the vitality of the cities and thereby incurring in-
direct responsibility for the gangrenous spots that appall
sociologists, parsons, and policemen. It is not so much that
suburbia has drawn away taxable values as that it has drawn
away intelligent leadership. A man whose bedroom is beyond city limits is not a city voter; and if he is replaced by

a man likely to vote less intelligently, the city has lost more than taxable values. Moreover, the man who vanishes with the setting sun will not come into intimate contact with many of the problems of the modern city, will not be chafed and harried by them, and so will not put his mind seriously to their solution.

The loss is incurred, furthermore, at the very moment when the tremendous shift of population is raising problems that tax our ingenuity, resourcefulness, and political competence to an extent without historical precedent. Just when the city needs brain power more than ever, many of its brainiest citizens betake themselves elsewhere. While this cannot fairly be called desertion under fire, it has the same effect. Sometimes the move is made for the one purpose of escaping city taxes; and in that case, it is desertion.

What this is doing to the central city has been pointed out by a thousand researchers in ten thousand books, magazine and newspaper articles, orations, seminars, television panel discussions, and other forms of publicity. But the researchers are for the most part gentlemen and scholars who speak in gentlemanly and scholarly language which is correct, exact, and urbane, but doesn't have much kick, and therefore doesn't make a clear and lasting impression. Gentlemen and scholars are intent on informing, not jolting. They describe the influx of population into the central city as drawn very largely from underprivileged groups in rural areas, trained in folkways consonant with their former environment but ill adapted to their new, which maladjustment produces socially deleterious results. That, they say, and not any biological inferiority, accounts for the civic inadequacy of this population. Which is no doubt an accurate description of what is the matter with these people, but it is severely rational, ignoring the emotional factor which, nevertheless, is important.

These newcomers are disliked because they stink.

The verb could be, but is not, used in a metaphorical sense, referring to the moral delinquency of many of the incoming group. The significance here is strictly olfactory. The reason is that sanitary measures, reasonably effective in the open country where they are powerfully reinforced by sunshine and fresh air, are not sufficient in a crowded city. Most of these people are poor, but that is not the answer. Many of them are Negroes, and some are Puerto Ricans, but that is not the answer. The answer is simply that they are not acquainted with the physical necessities of city life.

In any old American city you can find streets that have been inhabited by wage earners for generation after generation. These are poor people, but their streets are as tidy and as inoffensive to the nostrils as those of the fine residential districts. In Baltimore some of these streets are occupied by Negroes whose fathers and grandfathers lived there; and they are as unobjectionable as the others. It is neither race nor economic status—that is, any status above complete destitution—that makes the difference; it is knowledge of how to live decently in a crowded environment. A poor man can refrain from scattering garbage about, and can keep track of the trash-collection days as easily as a millionaire, provided he realizes the necessity of doing so; but if he has never had to do it before, it may take him a long time to learn.

That period of education is an affliction to the city, and when the numbers involved are large it may be a grievous affliction. Gentlemen and scholars tend to gloss over this point and emphasize the city's duty, rather than its bane. It is a noble attitude that attests their Christian charity; but it does ignore some of the facts.

When a city such as Baltimore, with less than a million people in 1950, finds that by 1960 it has lost 400,000 of its former citizens and had them replaced by 375,000 stinkers, it has a very formidable problem of education on its hands, and experiences considerable difficulty in doing its duty. This is a hard, solid fact, which ought to be taken into account.

Berating the newcomers, to be sure, is no help. These are all God's chillun, just as much as the rest of us, and that must not be forgotten. But if wrath is no good, neither is being mealy-mouthed. The fact that a man spreads about him effluvium that might knock out a goat at ten paces is no proof that he is biologically inferior to the gorgeous creatures who preside over the cosmetics-and-perfume counters in the big department stores. But he doesn't smell so good. That solid fact ought to be taken into account.

Nor is the problem confined strictly to sensory perception. Metaphorically, too, these newcomers stink. They carry their liquor badly; with even a moderate load on they become quarrelsome and they quickly explode into violence. They stand in no awe of a uniform, and to go along quietly with a policeman because he is the Law is foreign to their nature. When they go quietly it is because the cop is armed and muscular, and for no other reason—well, there is the additional reason that there are usually two cops to one hill-

billy or blue-gum buck. This attitude is by no means unreasonable in remote Appalachian coves, or Alabama cane-
brakes where the Law is ordinarily far away, and a man
who may be molested with impunity will not long survive.
But it is extremely wearing on the police force and policemen are expensive, hence it cannot be tolerated in the city.
The fact that the explanation is at hand and easily understood doesn't alter the other fact that when thousands of
such people come pouring into a city the total annual cost
of repairing and replacing police officers rises tremendously;
and it is this fact that interests the taxpayers.

The high incidence of the more serious sexual offenses—
rape, incest, perversion, and pandering—in this group is
also susceptible of an explanation that has no reference to
their place on the biological scale. Poverty is part of it, but
sheer bewilderment is probably a more important factor.
Most rural regions are fairly homogeneous. In the South
there is the division into black and white, but even that
doesn't extend to cultural and moral standards; black and
white in the South are pretty well agreed on what is right
and what is wrong, on what conduct is admirable and what
reprehensible. So when they come into contact with people
of widely diverse cultural ideas, as they must in a large
city, they are likely to misunderstand; they do not realize
that the standards with which they are familiar are rejected
because other people have different standards. Instead, they
jump to the conclusion that no standards exist in the city.

Basically, this is an error rather than a crime, the fruit of
a misconception more than proof of moral turpitude. But
that doesn't empty the jails, the hospitals, and the insane

asylums filled by the breakdown of sexual tabus. Nor does
it make it any safer for an unescorted woman to go to the
corner to put a letter in the mailbox after dark. That the
increase in the crime rate can be checked and even reversed
by intelligent measures of social amelioration is probably
true; but that is a development of the future and the incidence of crime is a condition existing here and now. Our
present methods of dealing with it are crude, but they do
have some effect. There is all too much reason to believe
that hanging one rapist doesn't deter another; but it effec-
tually deters the one whose neck is broken.

This is a fact that does not escape those citizens who go
in terror of their lives on account of the changing character
of the central city, and it causes them to regard theoretical
penology with a lackluster eye. In my own neighborhood
recently, by the arrest of two young degenerates, both with
previous convictions, the police had solved, at last accounts,
no less than sixty-seven crimes, ranging from purse snatch-
ing to two cases of rape-murder. The hard-headed, and may-
hap hard-hearted, figure that, if these two had gone to the
gallows for the first offense, the community would have
been spared five subsequent outrages, although the example
might not have reformed a single other punk.

Nevertheless, in moments of calm reflection we all know
that the bastinado and the hangman's noose are not the most
effective means of civilizing the Yahoos, and to civilize them
is the inescapable obligation of a civilized city. Education
alone will do the work, and education implies not merely
classroom instruction, but fair treatment, patience, and per-
severance outside the schools. The civic education of a non-

urban population is hard, dangerous, and expensive work, not the exercise in psalm singing, sermonizing, and tut-tutting that sentimentalists seem to think it is.

It involves fighting off the wolf pack that falls upon the countryman as soon as he comes to town—greedy landlords, conscienceless loan sharks, employers who are spiritual heirs of Simon Legree, and every known variety of swindler and extortionist. These are well equipped with fang and claw and they cannot be scourged from their prey without great exertion and probably not a few painful lacerations. It is a fatiguing and unpleasant business, and the smaller the number engaged in it, the greater the effort required.

Civic education involves also supplying the modern equivalent of the Roman circuses, entertainment on an appropriate intellectual level. The philosophical basis of this is the axiom that the man who is having a thoroughly good time legitimately isn't thinking up devilment. Yet it is notoriously difficult to secure appropriations from city authorities for parks, playgrounds, and other recreational facilities.

Recently I had the honor and privilege of voting for bond issues totaling twelve million dollars for the erection in my city of an arena suitable for wrestling matches and boxing bouts. Neither the cauliflower-ear nor the grunt-and-growl industry interests me in the least, and I expect never to set foot in the place. But there are many whose lives are brightened by watching such affairs; so a vote to provide them I believe was a vote to discourage more nefarious forms of entertainment. At the same election, I also voted in favor of nine millions for extension of an art gallery, but that was defeated, curiously enough by opposition from the presumably respectable element.

This heat and burden the refugees in suburbia escape and their defection has made the problem too much, thus far, for the men who are left behind. That is why the central cities have been steadily deteriorating until now their characteristic pattern is that of a business district surrounded by a ring of slums in various stages of disintegration.

What can be done about it? Well, let us consider first what, if anything, should be done about it. The suburbanite regards himself as well out of it, and if that is true, the case would seem to be closed. The invitation in the old folk song,

> Wake up,
> Jacob,
> Strike up a light,
> Help your daddy in a polecat fight,

seems rather pointless unless one can show cause for Jacob's bestirring himself. If the polecat fight is actually none of his affair, filial affection alone will hardly be enough to drag him out of bed. Suppose the central city does gradually rot away, will the suburbanite stand to lose anything of much value?

The question cannot be answered with a simple yes or no. It depends upon what the suburbanite is. If he is a straight Organization Man, it is hard to see why he should worry about the fate of the city, for the organization, not the city, is the center of his life. If the environment becomes intolerable, his recourse is to prevail upon the organization to transfer him to a better place, not to expend his energy trying to improve the one where he is.

No doubt the complete Organization Man is a rarity, but in suburbia a large proportion of the population bears that character to some extent. The great national corporation, now the chief employer of junior executives, is as innocent of parochialism as the army. Repeated displacements, often involving movements half across the continent, are normal occurrences in the lives of its employes. Indeed, lifetime residence in a single city is more often than not an indication of relative failure; as a rule the man who is never transferred to a new place has not advanced in the organization.

So what of it? Is it reasonable to advise a man to strike roots into the soil when the chances are that within five years, or ten at most, he will find himself transferred to the other side of the Mississippi, or to the other side of the Potomac-Ohio line? It is debatable, to say the least. Yet to write off these people as responsible citizens would be to write off an alarmingly large proportion of all the intelligence, energy, and resourcefulness potentially available to the community. As long as they are in residence they pay taxes, so the monetary loss may be neglected. It is the civic loss, the loss of effective citizenship, with which this discourse is concerned. Is there any appreciable loss of that kind?

In the estimation of a man who is left behind there certainly is; but that opinion, it must be admitted, is based upon a concept of the nature of a city that does not appeal to all minds. If the city is merely a place in which to make a living, then the desirability of one over another rests primarily upon economic considerations, some weight being given to climate, salubrity, and convenience. But if it is a place in which to live, then the economic factor loses some part if not all of its priority.

For life implies development, ordinarily growth, but always an increase in complexity of organization. Life is the great exception to the second law of thermodynamics. Time, in all the rest of the universe, may be a process of running down, but in that part which we describe as living organisms it is, up to a point, the opposite, the process of being, like a clock, wound up. True, at a certain point—not at a certain age, for the age is indeterminate—a man begins to run down, and he is then headed for death. But during his active life he continues to develop, and a successful life means development in desirable ways.

Intellectual and cultural development are admittedly desirable, and the city's justification of its existence is the historical fact that it affords facilities for this kind of development. Its libraries, its museums, its concert halls, theaters, and auditoriums, all its means for the interchange of ideas and opinions, compensate for its physical disadvantages, and since written history began have drawn into it alert and vigorous minds. These facilities are available even to a temporary resident as readily, generally speaking, as to a native.

What the man who is here today and gone tomorrow cannot achieve is participation in the life cycle of these things. I do not mean a contribution to them, although as a taxpayer the citizen does contribute. I mean the experience of observing them as they are established, flourish, and perhaps decline.

To visit an art gallery is, undoubtedly, to participate to some extent in that form of culture; but it is nothing like as deep a participation as to have visited the same gallery occasionally for twenty years, to have noted its new acquisitions, to have marked the shifts in popularity of various kinds of exhibits, in short to have acquired a proprietary interest in the place. You may never have given a penny toward its upkeep, but if you have given it your attention over a long period you have come into a sort of ownership, an attitude that no American has toward the Louvre, or the Prado, or the Uffizi. And what is said of the art gallery applies with equal or even greater force to the local orchestra, the local park system, and the local baseball team.

Long ago the declaration, *Civis Romanus sum*, meant a great deal more than identification with a geographical locality. It meant a kind of man, not a statistic in the census report. It meant identification with a historical process that, with all its defects, deserved Poe's one-word description, "grandeur." To regard it as a desirable status may be old-fashioned, but is not necessarily mistaken. Not all that is old-fashioned is erroneous.

We have been not without a touch of that kind of thing even here in America, although we are accustomed to hold it in more or less gentle derision. "Charleston is where the Ashley and Cooper rivers meet to form the Atlantic ocean." "Sir, Shakespeare was a great genius. There are not six men in Boston who could have written the plays of Shakespeare." All right, laugh; but laugh as you will, there is a small kernel in these jests that cannot be laughed away, some approach to the status of the *Civis Romanus* when Augustus ruled the world.

But granting, for the purpose of argument, that it is as desirable as the man who feels left behind thinks it is, another question bobs up. Is it attainable by the modern American? Not easily, that is certain. There will be no such inevitability about it as there was when many influential Americans could say, "This house, which my grandfather built, and in which my father and I were born, will certainly be inhabited by my son, and presumably by his son." That time is gone and as far as the future is predictable, not one American in a hundred thousand will ever again be able to make such a remark.

It does not follow, however, that increasing mobility has destroyed all possibility of developing the kind of civic consciousness that once was inevitable. But where once it came by inheritance, now it must be acquired by taking thought. It can be done and, in exceptional cases, it is being done. Most of us have encountered Organization Men who have spent thirty years of active life in half a dozen cities and have exerted a powerful cultural influence on every one of them. They are invariably extraordinary men, but not so rare as to rate being called phenomenal.

These are men who have developed an urbanism that is attached not to the City of Baltimore—or Boston, or Charleston, or Kalamazoo—but to The City. On any pavement they are at home; only when they tread on grass or clay are they alien. They are the hope of Megalopolis, they are the men who may have the wit, the wisdom, and the energy to cope with such a sprawling monstrosity as the Boston-to-Baltimore complex and reduce it to order, safety, and convenience, perhaps to endow it with beauty.

They are admirable. They deserve the praise and the hearty assistance of every patriot. They will perhaps develop a type of citizenship that, all things considered, will be superior to any type heretofore known. All the same, they are deprived of something. It is intangible, imponderable, and indescript; therefore they will never know that they lack it, which is perhaps just as well as it saves them from coveting the unattainable. But it is precious. It is the fervent glow that the sound of a name, Baltimore, Boston, Charleston, can set up in the breast of a man who at heart believes that his city's rivers form the ocean, and that three or four, if less than six, of his fellow citizens could write the plays of Shakespeare.

8

"THOU SHOULD'ST BE LIVING AT THIS HOUR"

WENDELL WILLKIE, who as a business tycoon was perhaps the twentieth century's most conspicuous example of the Displaced Person, gained fame, if not fortune, when he turned to his true vocation of political philosopher. But when he summarized what he had learned in that field he damaged his book by giving it an inept and misleading title, to wit, *One World*. He had in mind, of course, the unitary planet which is inhabited by all the physical bodies harboring diverse minds that compose the human race; and his aim was to alleviate the jostling attendant on such a situation by depicting and emphasizing the techniques made indispensable by the necessity of living on a single globe.

But it is not the unitary planet, it is the pluralistic world in which he finds himself, that worries the man who feels left behind. Obviously, we, and the Russians, and the Chinese, must needs live together on the unit that bears the name of Earth; and discovery of how to accomplish that feat with a minimum of organized murder is the immediate, urgent task of statecraft. To that point we may go along with Mr. Willkie without demur.

It is the assumption that statecraft may hope to accomplish its task by creating a single policy in the international field without a great deal of preliminary work toward creating a single mind among individuals that is doubtful, and becomes more doubtful whenever a President or a Secretary of State proposes some bold, new departure in diplomacy. Every such proposal encounters a chilly reaction from important segments of public opinion. Presidents and Secretaries of State in this democracy can take only such action as is consonant with the dominant tone of public opinion. In any field a bold, new departure implies self-confidence; and in the field of international relations self-confidence is precisely what the American people have most conspicuously lacked in recent years. So we have been forced into a policy that is, to a very large extent, a policy of drift; and in a critical situation no policy is more surely disastrous.

Yet time was when all outside observers agreed that one characteristic of the typical American was a self-confidence so towering that it amounted to an absurdity. Tocqueville commented on it tolerantly, Dickens and Mrs. Trollope acidly, Harriet Martineau and Fanny Kemble regretfully, but nobody missed it. Why is it missing now to such a marked extent that friendly aliens, D. W. Brogan and Jacques Maritain, for example, feel impelled to prescribe literary tranquilizers?

Every practitioner of political medicine has his own diagnosis, of course, and none should be accepted as infallible. But with that *caveat* entered, here is one that has at least the merit of plausibility: the man who feels left behind feels that way, and is accordingly uneasy, precisely because he does not and cannot live in One World, but must inhabit at least four. He is pulled first this way, then that, until his intellectual and emotional seams are strained and he tends toward the deplorable state that the savants call schizophrenic.

There are (1) the world of Einstein and Heisenberg and Teller, the world of advanced scientific thought, in which the typical American must live for two equally powerful reasons, first, because it may blow him up, and second, because it suggests a promise of release from the primal curse of Adam, "in the sweat of thy face shalt thou eat bread"; and (2) the world of plain common sense, which has been his refuge from time immemorial. Then there are (3) the world of competitive effort, which the poets have described as

> Nature, red in tooth and claw
> With ravin,

which is pretty extreme, but not wholly untrue; and (4) the world which has been variously described as the Kingdom of God, Nirvana, and Utopia, and which is frankly a creation of the mind, a vision—or, if you prefer, a fantasy—but which nevertheless is as real as the concepts of good and evil. He may be a citizen of any of the four primarily, but never totally, for he has relations with the other three and he disregards those relations at his peril.

The last observation is admitedly controversial and possibly heretical, but certainly not cynical. From Plato and St. John the Evangelist down at least as far as Samuel Butler, idealists have been exhausting the resources of rhetoric, poetry, drama, and the graphic and tonal arts in representing the glories and delights of the fourth world; and from Aristophanes to George Orwell satirists have shown equal vigor if not equal eloquence in portraying the woes and horrors of the third—with, as I believe, some effect. But that effect as far as it involves the transfer of human life in bulk from the realm of the competitive to that of the fraternal has been, let us say, nominal. It has spread civilization as a thin veneer over ravin, but it remains deplorably thin, and within the past fifty years has suffered so many ruptures as to shake confidence in the possibility of its permanence.

This tension, however, is old stuff and centuries ago men in general learned to live with it. Men in particular—as for instance, Americans—often find the ancient struggle between virtue and vice complicated by extraneous factors that increase its stresses. The democratic system, reposing ultimate power in the hands of the people, imposes upon us the obligation to live virtuously not only in private but in public life; as members of a self-governing community it is our task not merely to inhabit the *Civitas Dei* individually but to carry along with us the whole republic, including the bums, the punks, the hoods, and the tarts, as well as the saints, the sages, and the grave citizens.

This is obviously not to be accomplished in the near future, and the fact that it is necessarily a long job relieves it of any maddening urgency. Of course it does happen that an individual here and there finds the strain unbearable and takes refuge in Zen Buddhism or some other sanctuary of the mystics; but the great majority of us find it possible to repair to church on Sunday and pray, "Thy kingdom come," only mildly perturbed by the lack of indications that it is coming at any time soon. We have lived so long in both the third and fourth worlds that we are pretty well adjusted, or at least inured, to the dichotomy. Call it pharisaism, call it moral anesthesia, give it any hard name you wish, but the fact remains that tolerance of the difference between what we are, and what we know we ought to be is a stabilizing factor of great survival value. It keeps us hypocritical, but sane.

What has threatened our balance is the sudden necessity of making an equivalent adjustment between the first and second worlds, the world of advanced science—strictly speaking, of advanced technology, for pure science disturbs few of us—and the world of common sense. There are foreign countries. That has been a dictum of common sense unquestioned through all the thousands of years of which we have written records. There have been, it is true, endless argument and wide variations of opinion as to the right definition of "foreign." They have ranged from treating "foreign" and "enemy" as synonyms to Terence's *humani nil a me alienum*, but Terence was admittedly occupying an extreme position, not disputing the existence of the foreign.

But is a nation actually foreign if it has the ability to reach across the border and literally, not figuratively, blow you out of your bed and into Abraham's bosom this very night? Common sense ought to account it a close, a dreadfully close neighbor. "Nothing human is alien to me" is profoundly, and also terribly, true when one considers the many things that are strictly human, but less than admirable— murder, treason, and perjury among them.

As it relates to, for instance, Russia, the American sees

this and shudders; but as it relates to himself he sees it not at all, and purrs. Yet if he stops to think he must admit that by reason of the abundance of our resources and the industry of our hired hands, the American people, including you and me, will soon be in position, if indeed we are not in position now, to butcher more human beings in a matter of minutes than lived in the Mongol Empire when Ghengiz Khan was raging. We say, and without doubt we sincerely believe, that we have no intention of doing so, but who, besides us, knows it? We are human, hence murder, treason, and perjury are not foreign to us. As regards perjury, if any doubt had existed—which it did not—it disappeared in 1960 when we lied, and blithely admitted lying, about the dispatch of an espionage plane over Russia. As for murder and treason, they are among the capabilities of all mankind.

Our formidable task, therefore, is to make our protestations of nonhomicidal intent plausible to a skeptical audience that includes but is not confined to Russians—to persuade it that while we inhabit the first world, the one revealed by nuclear physics, intellectually, we are spiritually citizens of the fourth, the world of the gentle mystics. The task is, in fact, a double one, since we must first convince ourselves. In times of relative tranquility there is no doubt that Americans are a people disposed to live and let live; but in stressful days, incited by the fire-eaters, the Tom Paines, the William Lloyd Garrisons and the William Lowndes Yanceys, we display a different character and are capable of writing as murderous a chapter of history as any nation in the world.

It is a singular anomaly that our two most famous apostles

of peace, Woodrow Wilson and Franklin D. Roosevelt, protagonists respectively of the League of Nations and the United Nations, were both conquerors of terrific potency, destroyers of seven empires and commanders of forces that make the phalanx, the legions, the Golden Horde, and the *Grande Armée* by comparison little more than police riot squads. Yet there is historical consistency in it. David, the warrior king, aspired to build the Temple. Alexander the Great dreamed of One World before Willkie did. Sully, who introduced the idea of a league of nations into Europe, was the minister of King Henry of Navarre, not exactly a pacifist even after he became Henri Quartre.

Thus it is not logically inconceivable that the nation that was the exterminator of Iroquois and Cherokee, and the ruin of Santa Ana, Hohenzollern, Hitler and Tojo, may be fundamentally pacific. The difficulty is to make the rest of the world believe it, and the difficulty is not lessened when we are unaware that it exists. Perhaps the most striking mental aberration of the typical American is his inability to understand why foreigners can't see what an amiable character he is. Common sense ought to convince them—and right there we step on a land mine. Ours is only in part, and apparently a diminishing part, a world of common sense.

In this adventure all of us, the man who feels left behind no less than Oppenheimer and Rabi and Bethe, must accept and conform to what is, whether it makes sense or not. As the physicist must adapt his calculations to the irrational behavior of the electron, so we must adapt ours to the irrational behavior of the foreigner. It is difficult, and it may be dangerous, but it is inescapable.

The suggestion that you and I, and Joe Doakes who lives

down the block, must apprehend and conform our notions
to the nature of the world now being explored by the giants
of modern thought is sufficiently appalling, taken as a raw
statement. It is impossible, on the face of it. One who, under
the guidance of James R. Newman, the popularizer, has
skittered around the verge of such a subject as, say, symbolic
logic, and has been told that the line

$$f(o) : n.f.(n) \supset f(n+1) : . \supset . (n) f (n)$$

is the equivalent of a definition, several pages long, of
mathematical induction, is, let us say, reduced to melancholy, not to say despair. If to understand that is a necessary preliminary to knowing how to vote in the next election, then we must take to the hills, men, for the dam is
busted.

But of course it isn't in the least necessary. What is
necessary is a realization that this conglomeration of symbols represents the determination of a powerful mind to
communicate a statement in a way that will mean one thing
and cannot possibly mean anything else. And the second
necessity is to realize how admirable is this determination
to learn and to proclaim the exact truth. This is the aspect
of the world of modern science that you and I and Joe
Doakes must understand, accept, and apply in our own
activities. Its mysterious operational procedures may well
enough remain mysterious as long as we perceive, and share,
the scientist's determination to arrive at truth.

There is no difficulty in understanding why words will
not serve the purpose when one considers that in Webster's
Unabridged Dictionary the word "it" is given eleven defi-

nitions; for if "it" can be understood eleven ways, then all the words in the Democratic (or Republican, or any other) political platform can be understood in at least eleven hundred times eleven.

You and I and Joe Doakes grasp this. We drew the inference long ago that platforms that may mean anything actually mean nothing. But that is not true. They do have a meaning, all of them, and it is always the same, namely, that our consent as registered by our votes is essential to carrying out any governmental program, wise or idiotic, sound or fraudulent, honest or rascally. But since we have always known that, the platforms in fact communicate nothing, and what we learn we must and do derive from other sources.

It is in this independent search for information that we enter the world of the heavy thinkers; for the heaviest labor that Einstein ever performed was not in devising the theory of relativity, it was in getting rid of the ten thousand false ideas that would have led him astray, and had led astray all his predecessors. In this matter, you and I are not left behind. We may well wish that we were, and that the heavy labor of getting rid of ancient intellectual rubbish could be delegated to some great man, or to some Sanhedrin of mighty minds. But it can't be done.

The Communists can indeed evade it by lodging all power in the Kremlin, but that dodge is not available to a nation of self-governing freemen. They must pick their own way through a world in which technology has erased all lines of defense, challenged the very concept of strategy, and shifted the basis of security from military strength to intellectual agility. Forrest is still half, but only half right. "Git thar fust" remains part of the price of victory, but the rest is not "with the mostest men"; it is with the soundest idea, for a correct understanding of the modern situation outweighs the heaviest battalions.

But this is a generality that everybody will accept and nobody will find of much use. The puzzle is not the general idea, but the specific means of applying it. The art of government is not practiced by plain citizens, but by officials chosen for the purpose; then what step, if any, can the plain citizen take to effect improvement of the art in the United States? Short ballot, woman suffrage, direct primaries, initiative, referendum and recall, "get out the vote" campaigns—

> Myself when young did eagerly frequent
> Doctor and Saint, and heard great argument
> About it and about: but evermore
> Came out by the same door where in I went—

old Omar was talking about theology, but his words apply to politics as featly. The door through which the political inquirer comes and goes is the word "chosen" as used a few lines above. As civilized man is a tool-using animal, his first step toward any successful operation is choice of the proper tool; so the question resolves to this: What tools can the plain man use to effect the improvement of government in this country?

The answer is, politicians.

It is an answer that well may stagger not intellectuals

only, but businessmen, white-collar workers, and skilled labor as well—in fact, everyone who uses his brain to interpret what his eyes have seen. In the American vernacular the word "politician" long ago took on much of the coloration of an epithet, associated with all the woes of the country. Yet the answer stands, for the politician, like Coolidge and the singed cat, is better than he looks.

To a man who has spent thirty years in newspaper work no one has to point out the defects of politicians as a class. Every veteran reporter is well aware that behind an imposing façade X is a fraud, Y is a crook, Z is a pompous ass; and X, Y, and Z make up a large proportion of all elected persons in this republic. It is a fact of life, and to ignore it is to abandon the only possible basis for a realistic understanding of our situation.

But who made the politicians the shabby specimens that many of them are? God? Nonsense! "Allah, the Compassionate, the Merciful," is incapable of any such scurvy jest. The devil, then? Well, Satan, if any, no doubt helped; but the product bears the unmistakable marks of human handiwork. The politician is a product of his environment, and his environment is this world, not the next; and in this world the operational factor is its population.

The politician, "at least one long step removed from an honest man," is what he is because you and I and Joe Doakes will not suffer him to be other. We are constantly putting pressure on him for special favors, indifferent to the fact that he cannot grant us any special favor without denying his right to someone else. The defeat of the better candidate is an event so common in American elections that a candid observer must marvel that the republic has survived; and as a rule the cause of his defeat is a refusal to yield to the pressure of some special interest.

The republic has survived because the politician at his worst is somewhat broader minded and more competent politically than his constituency. Except at one point, ours is a representative, not a direct democracy. That one point is the polling place. When a man enters the voting booth he is responsible to himself alone—well, to God, if he is religious, but as touching strictly mundane affairs he represents nobody but himself and therefore votes in what he considers his own interest. If he is a wise man he knows that in the long run it is to his own interest to support honest and competent government; but none of us is wise at all times and lamentably large numbers are not wise at any time, which is what makes political freedom perennially dangerous.

The politician does not enjoy this freedom. At all times he represents, hence inevitably must consider, some interest other than his own, which means that his view is necessarily broader, by however narrow a margin, than that of the individual voter. Assume for the purpose of argument that he is a born lackey, utterly subservient to the will of some political boss; still, since there are always rival bosses, he must choose which one he will serve. Assume that he is venal, yet, like Pooh-Bah, he must determine who is likely to insult him with the more considerable bribe. But now assume—which in point of fact is far more often the case— that he has a distinct preference for being honest when it is not too inconvenient; then his training in habitually considering more than one interest is invaluable in helping him judge accurately what is genuine, not merely apparent, honesty.

The experienced politician knows better than anyone else how to run the country. By the same token, he also knows better than anyone else how to rob the country. Whether he will run it, or rob it, depends upon the relative strength of his larcenous propensities; and to estimate them is the task of the voter. In any case the man in public office, be he statesman or racketeer, can operate successfully only after he has mastered techniques that are far indeed from being instinctive.

This touches one of the most pervasive as well as one of the most dangerous of all the fallacies that the American people have from time to time embraced. Walter Lippmann has defined it as the fallacy of the omnicompetent citizen, but perhaps it is more vividly presented as the theory that when a man has proved an utter failure in every other line of human endeavor there remain three careers in which he may reasonably hope to succeed—he may teach school, edit a newspaper, or govern the state, for these require no sort of competence. It is this fallacy that supports the delusion that rotation in office is somehow of the essence of democracy.

The delusion is not confined to the unlettered. In 1960 Lippmann himself confided to a television mike that in 1948 he supported Dewey because he thought that the Republican party had been out of office too long and was therefore deteriorating. The Twenty-Second Amendment was not based entirely, as some have thought, on the age-old impulse of the live jackass to kick the dead lion, but, in some small measure at least, was a reflection of a quite sincere belief that it is somehow undemocratic to admit that special talent for the job qualifies a man to hold the Presidency although other good party workers want it. Enthralled by the beautiful theory that every American boy has the right, we ignore the brutal fact that very, very few American boys have the brains to be President.

But is this delusion characteristic of the politicians more than of other elements of the population? The evidence does not suggest it. On the contrary, every experienced politician is free of the delusion that just anybody can hold any job. Four times out of five he was cured the hard way—by suffering a backfire from the mistake of putting a nincompoop into an office that he couldn't fill. Politicians above the level of ward heeler are usually strong for the Civil Service because, in the matter of jobs, it takes the heat off them without compelling them to say right out loud that rotation in office, far from being its essence, is the ruin of democracy.

The flat truth is that when it comes to playing the role of a competent, responsible citizen of a self-governing country the typical politician is a long stride ahead of the typical voter; and this suggests the possibility that his immediate need is not further improvement, but a fair chance to use the capacity he has already developed. Not within living memory and probably not since the founding of the nation has there been a Congress that did not have before it more wise and salutary legislation than it enacted. The defeat of good laws is seldom, if ever, attributable to the incapacity of members to appreciate their excellence. The politician acts as he does, not because he knows no better, but because his constituents know no better than to demand that he play the giddy goat.

It follows that with no improvement whatever in the quality of the men holding public office the quality of government might be vastly improved if they were permitted to do their best. Theoretically, they ought to do their best anyhow, thereby committing political suicide. But they aren't going to do it. We know that they aren't going to do it. In their place we wouldn't do it. So to assert that a politician ought to vote for the general welfare against the wishes of his constituents is not idealism, it is unctuous hypocrisy, as contemptible as the worst acts of the jobholder.

The remarkable thing is the frequency with which men in public office do take chances in the interest of honest and efficient government. A measure that incurs the violent hostility of ignorance and prejudice but that enlists the support of the intelligence of the community usually has a good chance in any legislative assembly, from city council to Congress. This is not necessarily pure heroism, but is in part shrewd calculation. It occurs because politicians have a keen appreciation of the difference between the numerical and the effective majority. A segment of the population comprising probably not more than a quarter of the whole runs this country, always has, and always will. That is because not more than one man in four has any appreciable moral energy; the others, inert, are simply dragged along, accepting their ideas, their ideals, and even the major part of their emotions from the animate minority. The politician, aware of this, knows that for practical purposes two of the vital constitute a majority over five of the lifeless. Therefore he sometimes ignores numbers to string along with the vital.

If vitality and intelligence were inseperable, democracy would work almost, if not quite, ideally, but that, unfortunately, is not the case. The late Huey Long and the late Joseph McCarthy were both endowed with a moral energy hardly exceeded by that of any other two men of their generation; both had, in addition, great shrewdness, but the suggestion that either showed real intelligence is preposterous. They were, however, exceptional. It is the fact that intelligence is associated with the dynamic personality rather more often than stupidity; and so the republic has survived.

All of which sums up to the pleasing theory that government, staffed by personnel no whit better than existing officialdom, could be vastly improved. Plato was unduly pessimistic; we need not wait until philosophers become kings, or kings philosophers, to rid the state of most of its evils; we need only make the best of what we have.

But the pronoun is "we" and that consideration gives pause to soothsayers who without it might be quite chipper in forecasting the future of the United States. If the prospect of better government rested entirely on raising the moral and intellectual level of the politicians who operate it, the problem would still be formidable, but its dimensions would at least be measurable. The politicians represent a class, large, but limited, and to persuade any segment of the population to amend its ways is an undertaking that, huge though it may be, is not unimaginable, not one that "defies conceptualization." However, it is not better politicians that we need, but better use, starting with more discriminating choice, of the type we have now, which brings the responsibility back to that vague entity invoked by the first three words of the Constitution, "we, the people."

Now if there is any proposition upon which science, art, and philosophy are agreed it is that changes in the basic characteristics of a nation, if they occur at all, proceed with glacial slowness. This has persuaded many critics of American life—Mencken, Nock, Beard, for conspicuous examples—that the faults of democracy are irremediable. Furthermore, since technology is producing new and ever more powerful engines of destruction at headlong speed, it seems highly probable that those faults are lethal; hence any optimistic view of the future of the republic bears the semblance not of reasonable speculation, but of millennial dawnism, hardly to be entertained by rational men.

But, in the words of the famous aria from *Porgy and Bess,* " 'Tain't necessarily so." Basic characteristics may not change, but personality traits certainly do, sometimes with startling speed. If Saul of Tarsus and Aurelius Augustinus are examples rather too stately to be cited as illustrations, consider Ebenezer Scrooge. One may doubt that nightmares banished avarice from the soul of Scrooge without denying that its outward manifestation was thereafter restricted. When "in the fell clutch of circumstance" a man is dangled by the heels over the mouth of hell, he is a changed man, not, perhaps, in his basic character, but definitely in his conduct.

This is so much a matter of common knowledge that it is

embedded in folk maxims, for instance in the facetious advice
frequently offered maids and widows of a generation ago,
"If you can't be good, be careful." It may be idle to hope
that the typical American will become a better man within
the predictable future, but it is certainly within his power
to become a more careful man, and in the opinion of this
observer he is doing so. Since 1945 he has been suspended
over Hell Gate, with the rope visibly unraveling, and he is
perceptibly changed, mainly by the adoption of more realistic attitudes. Even in Iowa, by 1960, it was generally
admitted that Red China is not a fictitious creation of the
Money Devil of Wall Street, and even in Mississippi the
race theories of Mr. Madison Grant are no longer equated
with Holy Writ.

To be careful one must of necessity be somewhat realistic,
at least to the extent of perceiving in which direction danger
lies. The American has without doubt some distance yet to
go before attaining a reasonable approximation of political
realism; but he is on his way, even if some of his most
prominent leaders still persist in describing the quasi-reli-
gious movement of communism as a "conspiracy," and some
apparently hold that adjusting and readjusting the balance
of international terror is the practice of statecraft. There is
a fair chance, too, despite the conspiracy cult and brink-
manship, that we are moving toward political competence
fast enough to escape ultimate catastrophe.

It would seem, then, that the American who feels left
behind is actually cherishing an illusion. In point of fact,
he is appreciably ahead of most of the world, not of his
own volition, but by the thrust of events far beyond his

control. The trend of history has propelled him forward at a pace much too fast for comfort. What is left behind is his breath.

"I am glad to have lived at this time," remarked Adlai Stevenson in a private conversation where he had no reason to be other than completely frank. It was a striking comment, for the time was 1960, and the talk had turned upon the swarm of troubles descending upon the country at that moment. It was anything but a gay and jocund exchange, for nobody had any sure cures; indeed, discussion of each successive topic had culminated much in the spirit of the successive messengers reporting to Job: "I only am escaped alone to tell thee."

Why then should a rational man, and a wise one, profess pleasure that his lot was cast in the middle years of the twentieth century? Obviously because it is a time when tremendous events are impending, and his hope of achievement is greater than his fear of disaster. To the man of vigor, the man who is wholly, not merely half, alive, the hope of accomplishment is the justification for living, and the ultimate disaster is not defeat in battle, but to be compelled to live out dull days when nothing can be done, for good or for ill.

"Milton! thou should'st be living at this hour," intoned William Wordsworth, adding by way of explanation, "England hath need of thee." It is a reasonable explanation, but not the only possible one. In the United States of America we may as reasonably say to the author of the *Areopagitica* "thou should'st be living at this hour" because Milton would enjoy life among us at this time. Something is going to be done in this country and by this country very soon. It may be something great, or something ghastly, but it will be nothing trifling, nothing dull, nothing to be forgotten as soon as we forget who was Miss America of 1960. When things are to be done a man as stout-hearted as Milton is always glad to be alive, then and there.

So perhaps Wordsworth's line is the best advice that can be offered to the man who feels left behind. For if he can contrive to be living neither in the past nor in the future, but at this hour, he will be so busy that neither being left behind nor being shoved out in front will any longer matter at all.